《云南少数民族非纸质典籍聚珍·丝帛素书类二》
编委会名单

国家民文出版项目库项目

民族文字出版专项资金资助项目

云南少数民族非纸质典籍聚珍

云南省少数民族古籍整理出版规划办公室◎编

丝帛素书类二

和六花◎编著

云南出版集团
云南人民出版社

图书在版编目（CIP）数据

云南少数民族非纸质典籍聚珍 . 丝帛素书类 . 二 / 云南省少数民族古籍整理出版规划办公室编 ; 和六花编著 . -- 昆明 : 云南人民出版社 , 2023.10

ISBN 978-7-222-21688-4

Ⅰ . ①云… Ⅱ . ①云… ②和… Ⅲ . ①少数民族—古籍—汇编—云南 Ⅳ . ① K280.74

中国国家版本馆 CIP 数据核字 (2023) 第 026124 号

责任编辑：胡元青　金学丽　柴　锐
英文审稿：郝婧剑　和玉虹
封面设计：马　滨
责任校对：崔同占　周　彦　柳云龙
民文审稿：和丽宝（纳西文）　依旺的（傣文）
责任印制：窦雪松

云南少数民族非纸质典籍聚珍·丝帛素书类二
YUNNAN SHAOSHU MINZU FEIZHIZHI DIANJI JUZHEN · SIBO SUSHU LEI ER
云南省少数民族古籍整理出版规划办公室◎编
和六花◎编著

出版　云南出版集团　云南人民出版社
发行　云南人民出版社
社址　昆明市环城西路 609 号
邮编　650034
网址　www.ynpph.com.cn
E-mail　ynrms@sina.com
开本　889mm × 1194mm　1/16
印张　21.5
版次　2023 年 10 月第 1 版第 1 次印刷
印刷　云南出版印刷集团有限责任公司华印分公司
书号　ISBN 978-7-222-21688-4
定价　560.00 元

云南人民出版社
微信公众号

如有图书质量及相关问题请与我社联系
审校部电话：0871-64164626　印制科电话：0871-64191534

概说

我国是一个统一的多民族国家。在漫长的历史发展进程中，各民族创造并积累了丰富多彩的历史文化，留下了浩如烟海的古籍。这些古籍资料，从不同的角度记录中华各民族的社会进程、历史走向和文化内涵，从不同侧面反映各民族祖先的智慧、文明成果和气质风貌，是中华文化的重要组成部分，是文化传承的独特载体，是中华民族多元一体格局的真实映射。少数民族古籍是其中不可或缺、独具特色的重要部分。云南素有“民族文化博物馆”之美誉，各民族先民创造了卷帙浩繁的书面文献和难以计数的口传文献。这些少数民族古籍涉及的语言文种多种多样，记录的内容博大精深，载体形态更是纷繁复杂，有记载历史时期官方盟誓、功绩、先贤德行、颁赏、封诰等的金石铭刻，有描绘先民生产生活景致和认知的岩画，有刻写了经书、经文和神灵造像的石刻，有绘制于麻布之上的各民族信仰的神灵造像，有用铁笔刻写在贝多罗树叶上的贝叶经，等等。这些便是本套丛书所要收集、采录的少数民族非纸质典籍。

一

中国少数民族古籍（以下简称少数民族古籍）是指中国55个少数民族在历史上用各自的语言文字记录并形成的文献典籍、碑刻铭文和口头传承资料等。其内容涉及政治、哲学、历史、宗教、军事、文学、艺术、语言文字、地理、天文历算、经济、医学等领域。本套丛书收集、采录的少数民族古籍的时间范畴一般以1911年为下限，但由于各民族的历史特点和古籍存世情况差异，根据各民族古籍的实际情况，有的可以延伸到1949年。

少数民族古籍是中国传统文化的重要组成部分，是古籍学、文献学的重要研究对象。传统研究未对此作出全面、系统的阐述，直到20世纪80年代，随着各级各类民族古籍工作部门的建立，民族古籍工作迎来了春天。1981年，中共中央在《关于整理我国古籍的指示》中指出：“整理古籍，把祖国宝贵的文化遗产继承下来，是一项十分重要的、关系到子孙后代的工作。”1984年，国务院在转发《国家民委关于抢救、整理少数民族古籍的请示》的通知中强调：“少数民族古籍是祖国宝贵文化遗产的一部分，抢救、整理少数民族古籍，是一项十分重要的工作。”根据指示精神，从国家到地方都建立了相应的民族古籍工作部门，全面开展少数民族古籍的抢救保护、整理出版工作。我国少数民族古籍工作以“救书、救人、救学科”为己任，取得了丰硕的成果。然而，这项工作也面临着重重困难，走得异常艰难。随着社会日新月异的发展，少数民族古籍资源和古籍人才流失态势日趋严峻，少数民族古籍学科的发展又相对滞后，基础理论研究十分薄弱。同时，中国各少数民族古籍种类众多、卷帙浩繁，对于少数民族古籍的分类至今仍无定论。对“民族古籍”的界定，是一个非常重要的问题，观点众说纷纭[①]。这里，我们无意对此做系统梳理，只为明确少数民族非纸质典籍收录的范围。

在少数民族古籍抢救保护、整理出版工作中，特别是1997年以来，围绕《中国少数民族古籍总目提要》开展的全国范围内的少数民族古籍整理工作中，我们习惯性地将民族古籍主要分为两大类：一是有文字类；二是无文字类。有文字类的民族古籍又包括三个子类：一是用各少数民族文字及少数民族古文字记载的历史文书和历史典籍；二是用汉文记载的有关少数民族内容的古代文献典籍；三是用少数民族文字和汉文记载的有关少数民族

① 李国文在《云南少数民族古籍文献调查与研究》（民族出版社2010年版）一书的“前言”中对学界关于“民族古籍”的理解和界定做了较为系统的回顾。近年，也有相关研究做了一些讨论，观点几乏善可陈。

内容的碑刻铭文。无文字的民族古籍主要是指各少数民族在历史上口头传承下来的具有历史和文化价值的各种资料[①]。在《中国少数民族古籍总目提要》实施过程中，鉴于少数民族古籍文献载体形式的不同，又将少数民族古籍细分为书籍类、铭刻类、文书类和讲唱类四类予以收录[②]。其中，书籍类全面收录少数民族在历史上形成的具有古典装帧形式的书册。铭刻类收录石碑、摩崖石刻、墓志、鼎彝、哀册、金属刻、竹木刻等碑刻铭文。文书类收录各类告示、契约、传单、函告、函件、账单、抄件、公约、规章、执照、档案、书信、柬帖等文献资料。讲唱类则收录少数民族口头传承的有关民族起源、民族迁徙、文明起源等具有历史文化价值的神话、传说、故事、歌谣等。依据少数民族古籍文献载体产生的四分类法，用于《中国少数民族古籍总目提要》各民族卷的编撰是符合客观实际且行之有效的。与此同时，因此项工作涉及面广、持续时间较长，这个分类法影响力较大。但是，依据古籍的载体形式对民族古籍加以分类，可否将"文书类"单独归为一类尚可斟酌。何谓"文献载体"？《辞海》中对于"载体"一词给出了五层解释，其中一个"指承载知识或信息的物质形体"。顾名思义，"文献载体"就是文献的物质载体，纸、绢帛、布匹、木头、树叶、兽骨、石头、金石器物、兽皮等等都可作为文献载体。"文书"一词起源甚早，早在汉晋时期的史籍中即已出现，是指以文字为主要方式记录信息的一种书面文件，按其性质可分为对公文书和对私文书，各类告示、契约、传单、函告、函件、账单、抄件、公约、规章、执照、档案、书信、柬帖等皆属文书。从这个层面来说，文书是依照文献内容界定的概念。在云南少数民族古籍中，同为文书，也有不同的物质载体形式，有书写在纸上的，有凿刻在砖石上的。

此外，乌谷先生《民族古籍学》一书对民族古籍的概念及其分类颇具代表性，他认为："民族古籍就是指曾经在中华人民共和国疆域范围内生活过的各少数民族或正在生活着的各少数民族在历史上遗留下来的一切用文字、具有某种文化含义的符号（文字的雏形）及口头语言记录下来的文化载体。这种文化载体可分为四大类型，即原生载体古籍、金石载体古籍、口碑载体古籍和书面载体古籍。"[③]按照乌谷先生的分类，各民族在历史上留传下来的以竹简、布帛、纸张为载体的各种历史文献，包括用各种民族文字书写出来的书籍、

① 国家民族事务委员会全国少数民族古籍整理研究室：《中国少数民族古籍总目提要·纳西族卷》"序言"，中国大百科全书出版社 2003 年版，第 1 页。

② 国家民族事务委员会全国少数民族古籍整理研究室：《中国少数民族古籍总目提要·哈尼族卷》"序言"，中国大百科全书出版社 2008 年版，第 10 页。

③ 乌谷：《民族古籍学》，云南民族出版社 1994 年版，第 6 页。

档案、文书、诏令、户籍、契约、谱牒、信札、告示、乡规民约等都归为书面载体古籍。在众多的分类法中，铭刻类（或称金石载体古籍）、讲唱类（或称口碑古籍）按载体形式作为单独的一类没有太多的争议。但“铭刻类”和“金石载体古籍”因提法不同，内涵和外延产生了很大的差异，铭刻类涉及的物质载体更为宽泛、全面，不局限于金石器物，涵盖了石刻、竹木刻、骨刻、摩崖、器物等。铭刻类实质上已涵盖乌谷先生所界定的书面载体古籍和原生载体古籍的一部分，但“铭刻类”强调的是古籍的书写方式，而非载体形式。“金石载体古籍”这个类目的界定又略显狭隘，未将骨刻、竹木刻等载体形式囊括其中。乌谷先生虽另外界定了“原生载体”这个类目，“原生载体是指在一个民族的文字形成之初，用于记事表意被赋予某种特殊涵义的实物或符号。……我国各民族在自己的历史上都曾先后留下了大量有关刻木记事、结绳记事、实物记事等生动翔实的原生载体古籍”。[1]从这个概念来看，将骨刻、竹木刻归入原生载体古籍一类显然不合适。

综上所述，因中国各少数民族所处的环境不同、历史发展进程各异，少数民族古籍的载体形式多种多样，有的数量稀少却异常珍贵，有的历史上有过却早已佚失。用一种或者几种载体类别对琳琅纷呈的中国少数民族古籍作分类，难度巨大，难免挂一漏万，概括不够全面。我们选择以“非纸质”作为切入点，除了纸质载体以外的，具有有形实物载体的云南少数民族古籍都是我们收录的对象，意在将散布在各地图书馆、博物馆、档案馆等馆藏机构的以及散藏民间的，长期未公之于众的，又具有重要历史文化价值、文物价值和科学研究价值的云南各少数民族非纸质载体古籍汇编成册，公开出版发行。

二

云南是一个多民族聚居的省份，人口达5000人以上的世居少数民族有25个，除回族、水族、满族3个少数民族已通用汉语外，其余22个少数民族使用着26种语言（有的民族使用两种或两种以上语言），其中14个民族拥有23种文字或拼音方案（有的民族使用两种或两种以上文字），并留下了卷帙浩繁的民族古籍。据统计，云南散藏民间的藏文古籍、纳西东巴古籍、彝文古籍、壮文古籍、傈僳族音节文字古籍、白文古籍、普米族韩规古籍、傣文古籍、瑶文古籍等计有10万余册（卷）。其他如苗族、拉祜族、佤族、景颇族、布朗族、布依族、阿昌族、怒族、基诺族、德昂族、水族、独龙族等虽无本民族的古老文字，但他

① 乌谷：《民族古籍学》，云南民族出版社1994年版，第10页。

们靠口耳相传传承本民族历史文化，口传文献丰富多彩，创世史诗、迁徙史诗、叙事长诗、神话、传说、祭祀歌、劳动歌、生活习俗歌等数以万计。此外，有古老文字的民族中尚有大量口传文献流传。云南少数民族口传古籍达4万余种，内容涉及政治、哲学、法律、历史、宗教、军事、文学、艺术、语言、文字、地理、天文、历算、经济、医学等领域。

云南少数民族古籍储量巨大、历史悠久、载体多样，其中不乏非纸质典籍。依据现有资料来看，云南25个世居少数民族都或多或少拥有一些非纸质典籍。每一个民族都曾经经历过或正在经历着无文字的历史阶段，为便于沟通交流、传辞达意，随之萌芽了一些可用于记事表意的"实物语言"或"符号语言"，如结绳记事、刻木记事、树叶信等原生文化载体。在特殊文化场域中，这些原生文化载体被赋予不同的象征意义，随着人类社会的发展，特别是文字产生后，原生文化载体在群体中的实用价值逐渐被淡化，有的甚至消失在历史长河中。但在无文字民族中，这些原生文化载体的实用价值已远超其文化和文物价值。原生文化载体是否能纳入民族古籍的范畴，至今仍众说纷纭。鉴于云南各少数民族留存至今的原生文化载体数量不多，珍贵且濒危，本书亦做收录。在目前所知的十余万册云南少数民族古籍中，基于各民族分布区自然环境各异，历史发展进程各有轨迹，传统文化各具特色，民族古籍的载体可谓琳琅满目，布匹、竹木、兽骨、兽皮、金石器物等都在不同的历史时期成为不同族群古籍的承载体。这里，我们大体介绍一下非纸质典籍数量较多、载体较具代表性的几个民族的古籍情况：

1. 纳西族典籍

目前已知国内外收藏的东巴古籍有1000余种（内容大体相同的算为1种）3万余册，俗称"东巴经"，多数为图画象形文字写本，部分为图画象形文和哥巴文掺杂写本，极少数为纯哥巴文写本。其以宗教典籍为主，亦包括用东巴文书写的文书、铭刻和纳西族口耳相传的口头文献，内容涵盖社会历史、语言文字、哲学宗教、风俗习惯、文学艺术、天文医学等多方面，被誉为"纳西族古代社会的百科全书"。按其内容可分为祈福延寿类的《远祖回归记》《献牲》《神鹏和署争斗的故事》等，禳鬼消灾类的《鲁般鲁饶》《董术战争》《创世纪》《白蝙蝠取经记》等，丧葬超度类的《杀猛鬼和恩鬼，高勒趣招父魂》《人类迁徙的来历》《马的来历》等，占卜类的《大地上卜卦之书》《用巴格图占卜》《占梦之书》等，涉及舞蹈、医药、民歌等的《东巴舞谱》《医药之书》《民歌范本》等，以及独具地域特色的丽江市宁蒗彝族自治县油米村的阮可东巴经。

纳西族非纸质典籍中，最具代表性、使用最广泛、储量较多的，有绘制于木头之上的木牌画和布匹之上的卷轴画。木牌画是一种历史悠久的原始绘画艺术，是东巴艺术在萌芽阶段的作品，大多应用于大型祭祀活动。木牌一般长约60厘米、宽约10厘米、厚约1厘米，内容依照东巴画谱所记载的为准，按祭祀功能可分为神牌、鬼牌、门牌、还债牌、诅咒牌等。图像造型奇特，形貌古朴，线条粗犷，笔法豪放，自然流畅，具有先民原始艺术的特点。卷轴画，纳西语叫“普劳幛”，是东巴用矿物质颜料绘制于土布上的神像画，是东巴绘画艺术跨入发达阶段而趋于精熟的作品，有长卷、多幅和独幅等多种。每幅卷轴画主要画一尊大神或护法神，表现某个神祇及其所居的神界，用于东巴教仪式中，悬挂于神坛正上方，不同仪式所挂的神像不尽相同。具有代表性的卷轴画有东巴教教主东巴什罗像、东巴教大神依古窝格、战神优麻、阳神董神、阴神术神、萨依威德、神路图等。其中，神路图是东巴卷轴画中最原始、最有代表性的巨作，一般宽16—30厘米、长约15米。画卷分段连续描绘地狱、人间、天堂三个部分，绘有360多个人、神、鬼及70多种奇禽怪兽，被称为我国美术史上最长的直幅长卷，享有“古代宗教绘画第一长卷”之誉，具有较高的文化和艺术研究价值。神路图的内容、性质、用途大体一致，但因载体材质、颜料、绘画技法等不同，每一幅神路图都有独特的艺术风格。

2. 壮族古籍

壮族有自己的语言文字，壮语属汉藏语系壮侗语族壮傣语支，分南北两大方言。壮族文字在先秦时期即已萌芽，隋唐时期，壮族先民即用汉字记壮语，效仿汉字六书的构字方法创制了方块壮字，称“土字”或“土俗字”，并用古壮字来记录民间故事，书写经文、家谱、碑文、账务等，一批方块壮字古籍流传至今。古壮文古籍，壮语称“师摩”“师多在”“师雅”等，“师”壮语意为“书籍”，多抄写在用纱皮树树皮制成的纱纸上，或是用嫩竹、构树皮制成的者卡土纸上。壮族古籍种类广、数量多，有记录摩教仪式、经文、教义的《摩经布洛陀》《摩荷泰》《麻仙》《德傣掸登俄》等，有反映朴素世界观和价值观的叙事长诗、古歌，如《盘古歌》《卜伯》《摩则杜》等，有民间七言叙事诗《毛洪》《董永》《舜儿》等，亦不乏展现绘画艺术的《鸡卜经》及宗教绘画“莱摩”，内容涉及历史、语言、文学、艺术、哲学、宗教、天文、历算等众多方面，可谓博大精深、绮丽多姿。

壮族的非纸质典籍以岩画、骨刻书和绘画典籍较具代表性。一是岩画。今壮族分布区尚存数百处摩崖石刻。据现有考古资料，今壮族分布区有众多的原始刻绘艺术遗存，虽难于明确界定这些考古遗存的族属，但壮族先民是这些绘画遗存的创作者之一是确信无疑的。分布在文山壮族苗族自治州境内最具代表性的岩画，有麻栗坡大王岩岩画、丘北黑箐龙岩画、砚山卡子岩画、广南弄卡岩画、西畴蚌谷狮子山岩画等10余处，占地约5430平方米，有170幅400多个图案。二是骨刻书。云南壮族先民在器物、兽骨甚至身体上刻绘图案的历史由来已久，至今仍在部分地区传承使用，其中以壮族的骨刻历算器最为著名，文山壮族苗族自治州民族宗教事务委员会在境内先后发现58块骨刻。骨刻，壮语称“甲巴克”“瓦甲巴”，意为刻在骨片上的图纹符号、书籍，是原始先民推算日历、占卜的器具。兽骨上一般刻有人物、桌子、棺材、植物、弓箭、动物、干栏、太阳纹等图像，是一种兼具审美和记事功能的图像文字。三是神像画。壮族神像画众多，类型多样、作品丰富，隐含借“神”避邪的世俗观念，审美态度与情感交织。依据其内容、形制、用途，大体分为摩教神图长卷、宗教挂图和占卜绘画三类。其中，摩教神图长卷是摩教特有的宗教神图之一，由摩教祭司传承使用；绘于壮族自制土麻布上，形制为长卷竖幅，分栏作画，多用于丧葬仪式、祭扫仪式等。

3. 傣族古籍

傣族有本民族文字。傣文古籍多为刻本、写本、稿本和抄本，有贝叶古籍和纸质（绵纸、构皮纸）古籍两种，形制一般为梵夹装、经折装、线装，主要流传于西双版纳、德宏、保山、普洱、临沧、红河等州市的傣族地区。按内容大致有宗教类的《朗丝奢不仙宰》《杀鸡祭水神祷辞》《祭谷魂词》《招魂词》等，政治历史类的《泐史》《孟连宣抚史》等，文学艺术类的《巴塔麻嘎捧尚罗》《兰嘎西贺》《厘俸》，以及天文历法类、农田水利类、医药类、理论专著类、军事武术类、语言文字类、译著类等。

傣族的非纸质典籍载体多样、数量众多，最具代表性的便是傣族的银刻、贝叶经书和绘画典籍。其中，贝叶经是最具代表性的非纸质典籍。贝叶经，傣语称作“坦兰”，是用民间制作的铁笔刻写在经过特制的贝多罗树叶上。此外，傣族的壁画、布画等非纸质绘画典籍也较有特色。

4. 彝族古籍

彝族有自己的语言和文字。语言属汉藏语系藏缅语族彝语支，可分为东部、西部、南部、北部、中部、东南部六大方言区。彝族有自己古老的文字，汉文古籍称其为“夷经”“爨文”“罗罗文”等，现统称老彝文，每一个字形代表一个字义，并有不同写法。现存的老彝文有1万多字形，常用的有1000多字。历史上，彝族先民用老彝文撰写了大量的文献典籍和数量众多的金石铭刻，内容涉及政治、军事、哲学、宗教、历史、地理、语言、文字、文学、艺术、天文、历算、医药、卫生等方面。近现代流行于彝族地区的彝文古籍主要有纸书、皮书、布书、骨书、岩书、瓦书、木牍、木刻、金石铭刻、印玺等载体形制，其中纸书占绝对比例，包括抄本与木刻印刷本两种。现存彝文古籍达 2 万余册（件），手抄本较多，少数为木刻印刷本。云南彝文古籍可分为滇南彝文古籍、武定禄劝彝文古籍、撒尼彝文古籍、阿哲彝文古籍、宣威彝文古籍、罗平彝文古籍、北部彝文古籍七类。较具代表性的有传统宗教礼仪典籍《吾查》《们查》《指路经》《祭龙经》《祈雨经》《鲁资楠道》《脑斯古》《招魂经》《尼布木司》等，著名文学作品有《阿诗玛》《尼迷诗》等，创世史诗有《查姆》《阿细的先基》《梅葛》《阿黑西尼摩》《尼苏夺节》等，译文文献长诗有《董永与七仙女》《凤凰记》《木荷与薇叶》《唐王游地府》《唐僧取经记》等。

云南彝族非纸质典籍最具代表性的是彝文摩崖。如昆明市禄劝彝族苗族自治县境内便有一通我国西南彝族地区历史较久远、留存较完整的长篇彝文金石铭刻——罗婺盛世史摩崖，刻面高 206 厘米 ×80 厘米，镌刻于明嘉靖十年（1531 年），迄今已有 490 多年，记述了武定凤氏土司 14 代 350 多年间的兴盛史。

云南每一个少数民族都拥有或者曾经拥有过或多或少的非纸质典籍。新中国成立以后特别是 20 世纪 80 年代后，很多的非纸质典籍得到了抢救保护，有的收藏于各级各类收藏机构，有的陈列于各类博物馆，有的已有了相关的整理研究成果。但更多的非纸质典籍，如深藏山野的摩崖石刻正经历着风吹日晒、沧海桑田，有的还曾经历过灭顶之灾；如壮族骨刻散布民间、无人释读，研究者有意寻访亦难见其真颜；又如纳西族木牌因仪式物品使用禁忌、用完即毁，难寻旧物……如此种种不止是云南少数民族非纸质典籍的现状，也是少数民族古籍所面临的困境。

三

文化是民族的根脉，是人类的精神家园，是一个民族凝聚力、生命力、创造力的源泉，是国家强盛的重要支撑。少数民族古籍真实而生动地记录了少数民族的历史发展进程，蕴含着少数民族特有的精神价值、思维方式和非凡的想象力、创造力，是人类文明的瑰宝，是中国珍贵的文化遗产。在长期的传播交流过程中，少数民族古籍发挥着积极进取的价值取向和经世致用的社会功能。一部优秀的民族古籍作品，其在民族社会中的价值远远超出了一个学科的专业范畴，代表了一个民族在某个专业领域的认知，反映了一个民族的某个历史发展阶段，甚或承载、再现了一个民族的社会事实和历史走向。加强少数民族古籍抢救和保护，对于丰富中华文化宝库，全面了解中华民族的发展历程，构建平等团结互助和谐的社会主义新型民族关系，推动民族团结进步事业，具有重要的历史意义和现实意义。

中华人民共和国成立后，在各级党委、政府的领导下，经过几代古籍工作者筚路蓝缕的努力，云南省少数民族古籍抢救保护和翻译整理出版工作取得了显著成绩。本着“抢救为主，保护第一”的原则，抢救了少数民族文字文献古籍3万余册（卷），口传古籍1万余种，以《纳西东巴古籍译注全集》《中国贝叶经全集》《彝族毕摩经典译注全集》《云南少数民族古籍珍本集成》《红河彝族文化遗产古籍典藏》《云南少数民族古典史诗全集》《云南少数民族叙事长诗全集》等为代表的民族古籍抢救保护成果引起国内外的广泛关注。但是，于卷帙浩繁的少数民族古籍而言，目前的抢救保护、翻译整理成果不过是沧海一粟。初略估算，除已征集保管的少数民族古籍以外，云南仍有数万册（卷）少数民族文字文献古籍散存民间。由于保管不善或无人传承等诸多原因，许多散存民间的古籍难于做到活态传承，佚失、损毁现象严重，抢救保护迫在眉睫。就云南少数民族非纸质典籍而言，其现状尤令人担忧。部分可移动的、具有文物价值的非纸质古籍，多数已被各级各类机构、企业、私人征集收藏，这样的抢救保护最大化地彰显了此类古籍的文物价值，但这些民族古籍收而藏之后，原本在民间尚能活态传承的民族智慧结晶极易成为待在深闺无人识的宝贝；少量仍存于民间的，亦不乏寻访之人，各色寻访者在山乡村寨走访寻宝，有的甚至被倒卖流到境外。而诸多不可以移动的非纸质古籍的生境更是让人心生惋惜，这些承载着民族文化的石刻、摩崖多隐匿深山，常年经受着日晒雨淋以致文字符号或字迹模糊、难于辨识，或直接被人为损毁。石刻、摩崖受自然侵蚀逐渐消失，这是事物发展的自然规律，但对于民族文化而言是一个让人痛心的巨大损失。

我们在做这套丛书的过程中，也亲历和见证了数次痛心的时刻。2011年起，在云南省财政厅、云南省民族宗教事务委员会的支持下，我们一直在持续开展“云南省百项少数民族文化精品工程”项目《云南少数民族古籍珍本集成》。同时，按照《国家民委关于印发全国少数民族古籍保护工作“十三五”规划通知》的要求，“基本完成全国少数民族古籍普查工作。会同相关部门全力推进普查工作，摸清各地少数民族古籍资源。建立健全普查登记管理制度，构建普查登记平台，对各地少数民族古籍普查情况进行录入、统计、汇总，形成全国少数民族古籍普查登记目录档案”。本着“摸家底、建平台”的目的，我们在云南省范围内开展了少数民族古籍普查、采录工作。为此，我们访遍云南各州市的少数民族古籍收藏机构，走访古籍传承人、收藏爱好者，足迹几乎遍及云南全省。2016年，我们在迪庆藏族自治州调研时，迪庆藏族自治州藏学研究院的同志为我们介绍了州内非纸质典籍的留存分布情况，提到在维西傈僳族自治县塔城镇附近一个山坡上有很多藏文石刻。我们在电脑里看到了该院数年前实地调研时拍摄的照片，从中可以看到半面山坡都是石刻，都是一些有些年代的文化遗存。我们异常兴奋，因为这个石刻分布地和发现唐代藏文碑刻《格子碑》的格子村相距仅数里，又隐匿深山，难保不是一些有价值的非纸质典籍。遗憾的是，因此行我们未携带拍摄设备，心想留待日后再专程前来调研。未想此次擦肩而过，却错失了一睹其风采的机会。2018 年 5 月，我们组织了专业的拍摄、传拓人员前往迪庆州，一行人在迪庆州藏学院相关同志的带领下，经历修路堵车、徒步山林，风尘仆仆地来到那片山坡。可眼前的景象却让我们傻眼了，哪里还见得到石刻，只见坡头有一道高五六米的混着石头的土堆，下方红土里稀稀拉拉种了一些重楼。几经周折联系上村委会的同志，方得知该村为发展农业经济，特地请了推土机来平整了土地，这些石刻已经被埋到了土堆下。这只是我们在开展云南少数民族古籍抢救保护工作中经历的几乎不值一提的一件小事，这样的事情不止在迪庆，全省各地都在发生着；不止石刻、摩崖，纸质文献、丝帛素书、竹木简牍无不面临着这样的生存困境。倾心于民族文化抢救保护的人们深感痛心，却也深深地感受到，仅凭一个部门、一些群体去抢救保护，确实是势单力薄。基于这样的现状，抢救保护非纸质典籍确实是迫在眉睫。基于经费、人员、技术等各方面的制约，哪怕是采用最简单、最传统的办法，也要把这些文化遗存的影像留下来，供社会科学研究使用，同时呼吁全社会共同关注民族古籍的抢救保护。这是一件意义深远的事情，也是本丛书策划之初最真实的出发点。

长期以来，云南人民出版社对云南少数民族古籍的抢救保护、整理出版工作给予了极大的支持。2016年，将云南少数民族非纸质典籍抢救保护项目申报国家民族文字出版专项资金资助项目，并获资助。云南省少数民族古籍整理出版规划办公室于数年前就多次到民族地区征集典籍，了解线索，拍摄图片。经过数年的努力，由丽江市博物院、丽江东巴文化研究院、丽江市玉龙纳西族自治县图书馆等单位和一些民间收藏爱好者收藏的云南少数民族非纸质典籍最终得以在此书中整合出版。为收集这些非纸质典籍，相关人员付出了辛勤劳动，足迹几乎遍及云南全省。大量的原数据采集回来后，我们在典籍的分类整合上却遇到了前所未有的困难。云南各少数民族的非纸质典籍载体可谓琳琅满目，每种载体类型古籍的数量和质量参差不齐，作为丛书汇总出版既要全面涵盖具有代表性的非纸质典籍的载体类型，又要兼顾覆盖各民族的非纸质典籍；既要鉴别甄选各民族非纸质典籍的珍品、精品，又要尽可能地考虑民族古籍在民族社会中的情感价值；既要客观地收录古籍珍品，又要考虑每卷图书的体量和规模。几经求证，严格按照民族古籍学的学科分类对云南的非纸质典籍进行归类，几乎是不可能的。我们只能对倾尽全力收集到的非纸质典籍做个大概的分类，各卷再细分类目。少数民族古籍的抢救保护是一项长期的工作，不是朝夕之功。我们想全面呈现云南非纸质典籍的精品、珍品，在实际工作中会不断发现新典籍、扩充新的类目，所以丛书难免有不当之处，唯有祈求方家海涵、指正。

总的说来，本丛书是云南少数民族非纸质典籍的第一次集成和汇总。它将以往秘不外传的众多少数民族古籍珍品第一次集中展示于世人面前，不论学术价值、史料价值，还是传世、鉴赏、收藏价值等都具有诸多独特性，在保护各民族文化遗产、弘扬各民族优秀文化、增进民族团结、促进中华民族共有精神家园建设等方面具有重要意义。

General Introduction

China is a unified multi-ethnic country. Various ethnic minorities have created and accumulated rich and colorful historic culture, while leaving a vast number of ancient books and records in the process of long-term historical development. Recording social process, historical trends and cultural connotations from different perspectives and reflecting wisdom, civilization achievements and the essence style from various sides, these ancient books and records are an important part of Chinese culture, a unique carrier for cultural inheritance, and a real reflection of the diversified but integrated historical pattern in China. Ancient books and records of ethnic minorities are an indispensable and unique part. Yunnan has long been enjoying the good reputation as "Museum of Ethnic Culture". Ancestors of ethnic minorities have created voluminous written documents and countless oral literature. A great diversity of language record types are involved in the ancient books of ethnic minorities. The contents of the records are extensive and profound, and the carrier forms are more complicated. Besides, there are inscriptions recording the historical events such as the official vows, merits and achievements, virtues of ancient wise men, awarding and imperial mandate appointments. Moreover, there are cliff engravings carved on the cliffs to depict the production and living situations as well as the cognitions of the ancestors. There are also sutras and scriptures carved in stone, stone-carved statues of gods, and Pattra-leaf Scriptures carved on pattra leaves with the stencil pen (a cutting tool used in carving seals, etc.). These are the non-paper ancient books and records of ethnic minorities to be collected and recorded in this series of book.

I

Ancient books and records of ethnic minorities in China (hereinafter referred to as ancient books and records of ethnic minorities) refer to ancient books and records, inscriptions, oral inheritance materials and other documents of 55 ethnic minorities in their respective languages in history, contents of which cover politics, philosophy, history, religion, military affairs, literature, art, languages, geography, the celestial almanac, economy, medicine and other fields. 1911 is generally taken as the lower limit for the time category of ancient books and records of ethnic minorities. However, due to historical characteristics of various ethnic minorities and differences in the existence of the ancient books and records, some of them may be extended to 1949 in accordance with the actual situation of ancient books of various ethnic minorities.

Ancient books and records of ethnic minorities are an important part of Chinese traditional culture as well as an important study subject of ancient books, records and literature. In the past, there were no comprehensive or systematic explanations on such subject in the traditional research. Nevertheless, with the establishment of various levels and kinds of departments on ancient books of ethnic minorities in the 1980s, work of ancient books and records of ethnic minorities ushered in the spring. In 1981, the Central Committee of the Communist Party of China pointed out in *The Instructions on Sorting-out of Ancient Chinese Books* that "it is a fundamental task that affects later generations to sort out ancient books and records and inherit the precious cultural heritage of the nation." The State Council, in forwarding the notification of *The Request from the State Civil Affairs Commission on the Rescue and Sorting-out of Ancient Books and Records of Ethnic Minorities*, stressed that "ancient books and records of ethnic minorities are part of the precious cultural heritage of the nation, and it is a fundamental task to rescue and to sort-out them" in 1984. In accordance with the instructions, corresponding departments responsible for the work of ancient books and records of ethnic minorities were set up at the national and local levels to carry out the rescue, protection, sorting-out and publication of ancient books of ethnic minorities. Over the three decades past, relevant personnel responsible for ancient books and records of ethnic minorities have been taking the mission of "rescuing books, people and disciplines" as their mission, and achieved fruitful goals. However, this task is also faced with numerous difficulties, and it is extremely difficult to push it forward. With the rapid development of society, depletion of ancient book and record resources and the outflow of talents for ancient books and records of ethnic minorities become increasingly severe. Besides, the development of the discipline on ancient books and records of ethnic minorities is relatively backward, and the basic theoretical research is very weak. For instance, there are so many voluminous ancient books and records of ethnic minorities in China that the classification of such books is still inconclusive. Moreover, the definition of "ethnic ancient books and records" is a very important issue, but relevant opinions are divergent. ①Here, we have no intention to make systematical sorting, but just to clarify the inclusion scope of non-paper ancient books and records of ethnic minorities.

During the rescue, protection, sorting-out and publication of ancient books and records of ethnic minorities, especially since 1997, when sorting out ancient books and records of ethnic minorities conducted throughout the country on *Summary of the Catalog of Ancient Books and Records of Chinese Ethnic Minorities*, we habitually divide ethnic ancient books and records into two categories: literal and non-literal categories. Ethnic ancient books and records of literal category can be divided into the following three subcategories: first, historical documents, books and records recorded in the current and ancient languages of ethnic minorities. Secondly, ancient literature, books and records relevant to the ethnic minorities recorded in Chinese. Thirdly, inscriptions related to the ethnic minorities recorded in the Chinese and minority languages. Ethnic ancient books and records of non-literal category mainly refer to various kinds of historical and cultural documents handed down orally by the ethnic minorities in history.② In view of the different carrier forms, ancient books and records of ethnic minorities were further divided into four categories of books, inscriptions, documents as well as lectures and songs in the implementation of *Summary of the Catalog of Ancient Books and Records of Ethnic Minorities in China*.③ Among them, the classical binding forms of books and records of ethnic minorities in history are comprehensively included in the category of books; stone-tablet and cliff carvings, epigraphs, inscriptions carved on the sacrificial utensil, the elegy volume, and bamboo and wooden engravings are included in the category of inscriptions. Various kinds of notices, contracts, leaflets, letters of notifications, correspondence, bills, duplicates,

① In the preface of *Investigation and Research on Ancient Books and Records of Ethnic Minorities in Yunnan* (The Ethnic Publishing House, Edition 2010), Li Guowen made a systematic review of the understanding and definition of "ancient books and records of ethnic minorities" in the academic circle. In recent years, there have been some discussions on the relevant research, but the views have nothing to brag about.

② The Research Office of Ancient Books and Records of Ethnic Minorities for National Ethnic Affairs Commission: "Preface" of *Volume of the Naxi Ethnic Group for Summary of Catalogue of Ancient Books and Records of Ethnic Minorities in China*, Edition 2003 by Encyclopedia of China Publishing House.

③ The Research Office of Ancient Books and Records of Ethnic Minorities for National Ethnic Affairs Commission: "Preface" of *Volume of the Hani Ethnic Group for Summary of Catalogue of Ancient Books and Records of Ethnic Minorities in China*, Page 10 of Edition 2008 by Encyclopedia of China Publishing House.

conventions, regulations, licenses, archives, letters, notes and other documents are included in the documentary category of ethnic ancient books and records. The myths, legends, stories and ballads with historical and cultural value related to ethnic origin, migration of ethnic minorities and the origin of civilization and other oral inheritance of ethnic minorities are included in the category of lectures and songs. According to the four-classification method of the literature carriers of ancient books and records of ethnic minorities, the compilation of various ethnic volumes in *Summary of the Catalog of Ancient Books and Records of Ethnic Minorities in China* is in line with the objective reality and effective. Meanwhile, the classification method has great influence because of the wide scope and long duration of the task. Nevertheless, since ethnic ancient books and records are classified according to the carrier forms, whether books and records of "documentary category" can be taken as an individual category is still to be considered. What is the "literature carrier"? Explanations in five aspects have been provided for the word "carrier", one of which refers to "the material form carrying knowledge or information". As the name suggests, "literature carrier" is the material carrier of literature. Materials such as paper, silk, cloth, wood, leaves, animal bones, stones, stone implements, and animal skins can be used as literature carriers. The word "document" can be dated far back in time, which could be seen in the historical records as early as in the Han and Jin Dynasties. Besides, it referred to a type of written documents taking the written language as the main method to record information, which could be divided into official and private documents, various kinds of notifications, contracts, leaflets, letter of notification, correspondence, bills, duplicates, conventions, regulations, licenses, archives, letters, notes and other documents by nature. Seen from this aspect, a document is a concept defined by the content of literature. In the ancient books and records of ethnic minorities in Yunnan, there are different forms of material carriers, such as documents written on paper or carved or chiseled on bricks and stones.

Furthermore, the concept and classification of ethnic ancient books and records mentioned in *Ethnic Ancient Books and Records* by Mr. Wu Gu were quite representative. He believed that "ethnic ancient books and records refer to all the cultural carriers of ethnic minorities who once lived or are living within the territory of the People's Republic of China, which are recorded in words, symbols with certain cultural meanings (prototypes of written language), and in oral languages carried over in history. This kind of cultural carriers can be divided into four major categories, i.e., ancient books and records of original, inscriptions, oral inheritance materials and written carriers." ① According to the classification by Mr. Wu Gu, various kinds of historical documents passed on by the ethnic minorities in history with bamboo slips, cloth and paper as the carriers, including books, archives, documents, imperial edicts, household registrations, contracts, ultimatums, letters, notifications, township rules and folk contracts written in various ethnic languages, are classified as ancient books and records with written carriers. In the numerous classification methods, the category of inscriptions (or known as ancient books and records with ancient bronzes and stone tablet carriers) and the category of lectures and songs (or called as oral inheritance materials ancient books and records) can be regarded as separate categories according to the carrier form without many controversies. However, due to different names, the connotations and extensions of "inscriptions and ancient books and records with ancient bronze and stone tablet carriers" vary significantly. Inscriptions cover a broader and more comprehensive range of material carriers and are not restricted to stone implements, including stone, bamboo, wooden and bone carvings and cliff engravings, implements and other materials. In essence, the category of inscriptions covers part of the original carriers of ancient books and records as defined by Mr. Wu Gu. However, "inscriptions" emphasizes the writing modes of ancient books rather than the carrier forms. The category of "ancient books and records with carriers of ancient bronzes and stone tablets" is narrowly defined, which does not include such carrier forms as bone and bamboo carvings. Although Mr. Wu Gu further defined the category of "original carrier", "it referred to material objects or symbols provided with a certain special meaning and used to record events or express meanings at the beginning of formation of the written language of an ethnic minority... Each ethnic minority has left over a large number of vivid and detailed original ancient books and records relevant to record keeping of events through wooden carving, knot tying and record keeping with material objects." ② Seen from this concept, it is obviously improper to classify bone, bamboo and wooden carvings into the ancient books and records with original carriers.

In conclusion, due to the different environments and historical development process of ethnic minorities in China, the carrier forms of ancient books and records of ethnic minorities are diverse. Some are rare but extremely precious, while some have disappeared in history. It is extremely difficult to classify the numerous ancient books and records of ethnic minorities in China with one or several carrier forms. Besides, it is hard to make comprehensive

① Wu Gu: *Studies on Ethnic Ancient Books and Records*, Edition 1994 by Yunnan Ethnic Publishing House, P6 .

② Wu Gu: *Studies on Ethnic Ancient Books and Records*, Edition 1994 by Yunnan Ethnic Publishing House, P10 .

generalizations. We choose the "non-paper" carrier forms as the point of penetration. In addition to paper carriers, ancient books and records with tangible physical carriers of ethnic minorities in Yunnan are all the objects to be included by us, for the purpose of compiling and publishing the ancient books with non-paper carriers of various ethnic minorities in Yunnan, which are scattered in libraries, museums, archive centers and other collection institutions in various regions, as well as the scattered folk collections, which have not been made public for a long time and have significant historical and cultural value, as well as value of cultural relics and scientific research.

II

Yunnan is a province where multiple ethnic minorities live in compact communities. 25 ethnic minorities with a population of more than 5,000 people have been living there for generations. Chinese is generally used in the three ethnic minorities (the Hui Ethnic minority, the Shui Ethnic minority and Manchu). However, the other 22 ethnic minorities use 26 languages (some ethnic minorities even use two or more languages). Among them, 14 ethnic minorities have 23 kinds of writing or spelling systems, and some of them use two or more written languages. Moreover, they have left over voluminous ethnic ancient books and records. According to the statistics, there are more than 100,000 books (volumes) of ancient books and records scattered in Yunnan, including those in Tibetan, Naxi Dongba, Yi, Zhuang characters, Lisu and Bai characters, Hangui characters in the Pumi Ethnic Minority, and Dai and Yao characters. As for other ethnic minorities such as the Miao, he Lahu, the Wa, the Jingpo, the Bulang, the Buyi, the Achang, the Nu, the Jinuo, the De'ang, the Shui and the Dulong Ethnic Minorities, although they don't have their own ancient languages, they pass on their historic culture orally, with rich and colorful oral documents. Moreover, there are tens of thousands of creation epics, migration epics, narrative poems, myths, legends, sacrifice songs, labor songs, living custom songs, etc. Furthermore, there are still a large number of oral literatures passed down among the ethnic minorities with ancient languages. There are over 40,000 kinds of oral ancient records passed on in the ethnic minorities Yunnan, covering politics, philosophy, law, history, religion, military affairs, literature, art, language, writing, geography, astronomy, calendar, economy, medicine and other fields.

The ancient books and records of ethnic minorities in Yunnan have been provided with the characteristics of huge reserves, long history and various carriers, among which there are lots of non-paper ancient books and records. All the ethnic minorities once experienced or are experiencing a period of history without written languages. In order to facilitate communication and convey meanings, some "material languages" or "symbol languages" that can be used to record events and convey meanings were created, for instance, the original cultural carriers such as record-keeping through knots tying, wood carving and with leaf letters. Under the special cultural circumstances, these original cultural carriers were provided with different symbolic meanings. With the development of human society, especially after the creation of the written languages, the practical value of the original cultural carriers in the groups is gradually diluted, and some even disappeared in history. However, the practical value of these original cultural carriers has far exceeded their cultural and historical-relic value. Whether the original cultural carriers can be included into the category of ethnic ancient books and records is still controversial. In view of the fact that the number of original cultural carriers retained in various ethnic minorities in Yunnan is limited, precious and endangered they are also included in this book. Based on the different natural environment in the distribution areas of various ethnic minorities, the distinctive historical development process, and the unique traditional culture, it can be said that there are a wide variety of the carriers for the over 100,000 discovered ancient books and records of ethnic minorities in Yunnan. Cloths, bamboos, animal bones and skins, ancient bronzes and stone tablet implements and other materials have become the carriers of ancient books and records of various ethnic minorities in different historical periods. Here, we generally introduce the ancient books and records of several ethnic minorities with a large number of non-paper ancient books and records as well as the representative carriers.

1. Ancient Books and Records of the Naxi Ethnic Minority

Currently, there are more than 1,000 kinds (over 30,000 volumes) of Dongba ancient books and records collected at home and abroad (books of roughly the same contents are taken as one kind), commonly known as "Dongba Scriptures". Besides, most are pictorial hieroglyphic-writing transcripts; some are mixed with pictorial pictographs and Geba scripts; a very few are pure Geba scripts. There are mainly ancient religious books and records, and documents and inscriptions in Dongba characters, and oral documents passed down from mouth to mouth by the Naxi Ethnic Minority are also included. Contents of the Dongba ancient books and records cover social history, language, philosophy, religion, customs, literature and art, astronomy, medicine and other fields, which can be regarded as "the encyclopedia of the ancient Naxi Ethnic Minority". According to the contents, the ancient books and records can be divided into the category of praying for prolonged life including *The Return of Remote Ancestors, Animal Sacrifice, Battle between the Great Roc and the Shu Synopsis*, the category of ghosts and disaster elimination such as *Luban Lurao, The War between the "Dong" and "Su"Tribes, The Creation, White Bat's Collection of Scriptures*, the category of the release of the souls from suffering in the funerals such as *Killing the Devil Ghost and Helpful Ghost, Gao Lequ Recall of Father's Soul, The Origin of Human Migration*, and *The Origin of Horses*, the category of divination such as *The Book of the Divination of the Earth, Divination with Hatem Bagato*, and *The Skills of Divination by Interpreting Dreams*, and the category concerning dance, medicine and folk songs such as *Dongba Dance Notation, The Book of Medicine*, and *the Model of Folk Songs*, as well as the Ruanke Dongba Scripture with unique regional features at Youmi Village in Ninglang County of Lijiang City.

Among the Naxi non-paper ancient books and records, the most representative, the most widely used and the most abundant ones are the wooden-plaque paintings on wooden plaques and the scroll paintings on cloth. As a kind of primitive painting art with a long history, the wooden-plaque paintings is a work of Dongba art in its infancy stage, which is mostly used in large-scale sacrificial activities. Generally, the wooden plaques are approximately 60 cm in length, 10 cm in width and 1 cm in thickness, and the contents are in accordance with the records of Dongba picture copybooks. According to the sacrificial functions, they can be divided into god and ghost plaques, door plates, debt-collecting, cursing and other plaques. The picture is peculiar in shape, simple in appearance, straightforward in line, and bold, natural and fluent in brushwork, which is provided with the primitive art characteristics of the ancestors. Scroll paintings, known as "Pulaozhang" in Naxi Language, are statues of gods painted on homespun cloth by Dongba people with mineral pigments, and are all works tending to be sophisticated when the Dongba paintings have entered a developed stage, including multiple types such as long scrolls, multiple and single pieces. A great god or guardian god is mainly depicted in each scroll painting representing a certain god and the divine circle where it lived. The painting is used in Dongba religious rituals and directly hung above the altar. Different statues of gods are hung in different ceremonies. Representative scroll paintings include statues of Dingbasheluo (founder of the Dongba Religion), Yiguwoge (great god of the Dongba Religion), Youma (god of wars), God Dong (god of Yang), God Shu (god of Yin), Sayiweide and Road Maps of Gods. Among them, the painting of the road to heaven are the most original and representative masterpiece in Dongba scroll paintings, with a width of 16~30 cm and a length of approximately 15 meters. Three parts of the hell,the world of mortals and the heaven are successively depicted on the scroll paintings, with more than 360 individuals, gods, ghosts and over 70 kinds of odd birds and monsters. It is known as the longest straight scroll in the history of the Chinese art, and enjoys the reputation of "the first long scroll of the ancient religious painting", which is provided with high cultural and artistic research value. The contents, nature and use of road maps of gods are basically consistent. However, due to different carrier materials, pigments and painting techniques, each the painting of the road to heaven has its unique artistic style.

2. Ancient Books and Records of the Zhuang Ethnic Minority

The Zhuang Ethnic Minority has its own language and characters, and Zhuang Language is a category of the Zhuang-Dai language branch of the Zhuang-Dong Group of Sino-Tibetan Languages, divided into two big dialects of the north and south. Zhuang Language was already in the embryonic stage in the Pre-Qin Period. In the Sui and Tang Dynasties, ancestors of the Zhuang Ethnic Minority recorded Zhuang Language with Chinese characters, and invented the square Zhuang characters, called as "Tuzi"or "Tusuzi". Besides, they used ancient Zhuang characters to record folk stories, and record scriptures, genealogy, inscriptions, accounting, etc. Besides, a batch of ancient books in square Zhuang characters has been handed down. Ancient Zhuang books and records are known as "Shimo", "Shiduozai", "Shiya", etc. in Zhuang Language. "Shi" in Zhuang Language refers to "books", which are mainly transcribed on the gauze paper made of barks of the Shapi trees, written on the Zheka paper made from fresh bamboos or tapa. The ancient books of the Zhuang Ethnic Minority are in a wide variety and a large number, including books recording the rites, scriptures and doctrines of the Mo Religion such as *Buluotuo Lection, Mohetai, Maxian,* and *De Dai Shan Deng E,* narrative poems and ancient songs reflecting simplicity world view and values such as *Pangu Song, Bubo,* and *Mozedu,* folk seven-character narrative poems such as *Maohong, Dongyong* and *Shun'er*. Moreover, there are also quite a few *Jibu Scriptures* representing art of painting as well as the religious painting "Laimo", contents of which cover history, language, literature, art, philosophy, religion, astronomy, calendar and many other fields and can be said to be extensive and profound and gorgeous.

The non-paper ancient books and records of the Zhuang Ethnic Minority are represented by cliff engravings, bone carvings and drawing books and records. The first category is cliff engravings. There are hundreds of cliff engravings in the current distribution area of the Zhuang Ethnic Minority. According to the existing archaeological data, there are many original carved and painted art relics in the distribution area of today's Zhuang Ethnic Minority. Although it is difficult to clearly define the ethnic group of these archaeological relics, it is certain that the ancestors of the Zhuang Ethnic Minority are the creators of these paintings. The most representative cliff engravings are distributed in the Zhuang and Miao Autonomous Prefecture of Wenshan. There are 11 places (12 locations), including the cliff engravings on the Dawang Cliff in the Malipo, Heiqinglong in Qiubei, Kazi in the Yanshan, Nongka in Guangnan and the Shizi Mountain in Benggu of Xichou, covering an area of approximately 5,430 square meters, with more than 170 engravings and over 400 designs. The second type is bone-carved books. The ancestors of the Zhuang Ethnic Minority in Yunnan had a long history of carving patterns on utensils, animal bones and even human body, which are still passed on and used in some areas. Among them, the most famous one is bone-carved almanac calculator in the Zhuang Ethnic Minority. The Committee of Ethnic and Religious Affairs of Zhuang and Miao Autonomous Prefecture of Wenshan discovered 58 bone carvings within its territory. Bone carvings, known as "Jiabake" and "Wajiaba" in Zhuang Language, refer to graphic symbols and books engraved on the bone pieces, which were the utensils used by the primitive people for calculating calendars and divination. Animal bones were usually engraved with figures, tables, coffins, plants, bows and arrows, animals, dry railings, sun patterns and other images, which are pictographs with both aesthetic and memory functions. The third type refers to the statues of gods. Majority of the engravings in the Zhuang Ethnic Minority are statues of gods, with diverse types and abundant works, implying the secular concept of avoiding evil by the power of "god". The aesthetic attitude and emotion are intertwined. According to its content, shapes and use, it can be roughly divided into three categories: long-scroll statues of gods in the Mo Religion, religious wall pictures and divination paintings. Among them, long-scroll statues of gods in the Mo Religion are among the unique religious images of the religion, which is inherited and used by the priests in the Mo Religion. Painted on the homespun linen, the statues are in long vertical-scroll form. Besides, column painting are made, mostly used for funeral and tomb-sweeping ceremonies.

3. Ancient Books of the Dai Ethnic Minority

The Dai Ethnic Minority has its own ethnic written language. Most of the ancient books and records in the Dai Language are carving and writing copies, manuscripts and transcripts. There are two kinds of ancient books and records, i.e., pattra-leaf and paper (tissue and vellum paper) books. The shape and structure are generally composed of the form of two plaques sandwiched together, folding and traditional thread binding, which are mainly spread in the Dai areas of Xishuangbanna, Dehong, Baoshan, Pu 'er, Lincang, Honghe and other prefectures and cities. According to the contents, ancient books of Dai Language can be divided into the religious category such as *Lang Si She Bu Xian Zai, Prayer for Chicken Sacrifice to the Water God, Prayer for the Soul of the Rice Sacrifice,* and *The Conjuring Words,* the political and historical category such as *The Le History* and *Xuanfu History of Menglian,* the literature and art category including *Batamaga Pengshangluo, Lan Ga Xi He,* and *Li Feng,* as well as the categories of astronomy and calendar, farmland water conservancy, medicine, theory monograph, military martial arts, language and characters, translation and other categories.

Non-paper ancient book carriers of the Dai Ethnic Minority are provided with the characteristics of a variety of forms and large quantities, the most representative of which are the silverware, pattra-leaf scriptures and ancient painting books of the Dai Ethnic Minority. Among them, pattra-leaf scriptures are the most typical non-paper ancient books and records. The pattra-leaf scriptures, known as "Tanlan" in Dai Language, are carved on specially-made pattra leaves with the stencil pen (a cutting tool used in carving seals, etc.) by local people. Furthermore, wall and cloth paintings and other non-paper painting books and records are also quite distinctive.

4. Ancient Books of the Yi Ethnic Minority

The Yi Ethnic Minority has its own language and writing system. Yi Language is a category of the Yi language branch of the Tibeto-Burman Group of Sino-Tibetan Languages, divided into six big dialects of the east, west, south, north, central and southeast regions. The Yi Ethnic Minority has its own ancient writing system, which was called "Yi Scriptures" "Cuan characters", "Luoluo characters", etc. in ancient Chinese books and records. Currently, they are collectively known as "ancient Yi Language". Each character pattern represents a literal meaning, and there are various ways of writing. There are over 10,000 character forms in the existing ancient Yi character, with over 1,000 words in common use. In history, ancestors of the Yi Ethnic Minority used ancient Yi Language to write voluminous literature and books as well as numerous inscriptions, covering politics, military affairs, philosophy, religion, history, geography, language, writing system, literature, art, astronomy, calendar, medicine, health and other fields. The ancient Yi books and records popular in the Yi Ethnic Minority in modern times mainly include paper, leather, cloth, bone, cliff, wooden slips, wood engraving, inscriptions, seals and other carrier forms, of which, paper books account for an absolute proportion, including transcripts and wood-carving printed copies. There are over 20,000 volumes (pieces) of ancient books and records in Yi Language in existence, a majority of which are transcripts and minority are wood-carving printed copies. There are over 20,000 volumes (pieces) of ancient books and records in Yi Language in existence. Ancient Books and records in Yi Language in Yunnan can be divided into ancient books and records in Yi Language in South Yunnan, Luquan and Wuding, Sani, Azhe, Xuanwei,

Luoping and the north. The more representative books include the traditional religious ritual ancient books such as *Wucha, Mencha, The Scripture for Guiding passage,* The *Scripture for Dragon Worship, The Scripture for Prayer to the Heaven for Rain, Lu Zi Nan Dao, Nao Si Gu, The Scripture for Recalling the Soul of the Dead,* and *Ni Bu Mu Si,* the famous literary work such as *Ashima* and *Nimi Poem,* the creation epics such as *Chamu, Axi's xianji, Meige, Ahei Xinimo,* and *Ni Su Duo Jie,* and the literature long poems in translation such as *Dong Yong and Qi Xiannü Celestial, The Phoenix, Muhe and Weiye , Tangwang's Wandering to the Other World,* and *Tang Monks' Journey for Buddhist Scriptures.*

The most representative non-paper ancient books and records of the Yi Ethnic Minority in Yunnan are cliff engravings in Yi Language. For instance, the Cliff Engraving Depicting History of the Flourishing Age of Luowu (the carved area is 206cm×80cm in height) is the long-piece inscription in Yi Language with a relatively large history and retained relatively complete in the Yi Ethnic Minority in the southwest region of China within the territory of Yi and Miao Autonomous County in Luquan of Kunming City, which was engraved in the 10th year during the reign of Emperor Jiajing of the Ming Dynasty (1531A. D.). It has a history of over 490 years, recording the prosperous history of 14 generations of Feng's hereditary headmen in Wuding in more than 350 years.

Each ethnic minority in Yunnan has or once had more or less non-paper ancient books and records. Since the establishment of the People's Republic of China, especially in the 1980s, many non-paper ancient books and records have been rescued and protected. Some are preserved in various collection institutions at all levels, some are displayed in various kinds of museums, and some have received relevant research results. Nevertheless, a great many non-paper ancient books and records, such as cliff engravings hidden in the deep mountains are exposed to the weather, have been changed a lot, or even have disappeared. For instance, bone carvings in the Zhuang Ethnic Minority were scattered here and there, and no one has interpreted them. The investigators intended to seek and discover the profound mysteries, but they failed. For another example, due to the taboo of using ritual items, wooden plaques were destroyed immediately after use, it is difficult to find the ancestors' utensils ... All these are not only the existing situation faced by the non-paper books and records of ethnic minorities in Yunnan, but also the dilemma faced by the ancient records of ethnic minorities.

III

Culture is the root of the ethnic groups, the spiritual home of mankind, the source of a nation's cohesion, vitality and creativity, and an important support for a strong and prosperous country. The ancient books and records of ethnic minorities are true and vivid records of the historical development process of ethnic minorities, which contain the unique spiritual values, ways of thinking and extraordinary imagination and creativity of ethnic minorities. They are the treasures of human civilization and the precious cultural heritage of China. Ancient books and records of ethnic minorities have been playing an active value orientation role and a social function of practical application in the long process of spreading and communication. The value of an excellent work of ethnic ancient books and records in the national society goes far beyond the professional scope of a discipline, representing the cognition of a nation in a certain professional field, reflecting a certain historical development stage of a nation, or even bearing and representing the social facts and historical trend of a nation. It is important historical and practical significance to strengthen the rescue and protection of ancient books and records of ethnic minorities for enriching the treasure house of Chinese culture, comprehensively understanding the development course of the Chinese nation, building a new socialist ethnic relationship of equality, solidarity, mutual assistance and harmony, and promoting the cause of ethnic unity and progress.

After the establishment of the People's Republic of China, under the leadership of party committees and governments at all levels, remarkable achievements have been made in the rescue, protection, translation, collation and publication of ancient books and records of ethnic minorities in Yunnan Province through unremitting efforts of several generations of relevant working personnel on ancient books and records. Based on the principle of "rescue orientation, and protection first", more than 30,000 ancient books (volumes) of written literature and over 10,000 oral ancient records of ethnic minorities have been rescued. Moreover, *Complete Works of Translations and Annotations on Ancient Books and Records of Naxi Dongba*, *Complete Works of Chinese Pattra-leaf Scriptures*, *Integration of Rare Editions of Ancient Books and Records of Ethnic Minorities in Yunnan*, *Reservation of Ancient Books and Records of Cultural Heritage of the Yi Ethnic Minority in Honghe*, *Complete Works of Classical Epics of Ethnic Minorities in Yunnan*, *Complete Works of Narrative Poems of Ethnic Minorities in Yunnan* and other representative ethnic ancient book and record achievements have attracted extensive attentions at home and abroad. However, the current achievements of the rescue, protection, translation and compilation are not worth mentioning for the voluminous ancient books and records of ethnic minorities. It is roughly estimated that in addition to the collected and preserved ancient books and records of ethnic minorities, there are still tens of thousands ancient books (volumes) of the ethnic minority literature scattered in Yunnan. Due to numerous reasons such as improper preservation or no inheritance, it is difficult to carry out active-state inheritance for many ancient books scattered among the people. Moreover, many ancient books are lost or damaged, so the rescue and protection task is urgent. The specific regional conditions of the non-paper ancient books and records of ethnic minorities in Yunnan are especially worrying. The majority of part of the movable, non-paper ancient books with cultural relic value have been collected and preserved by the institutions at all levels, enterprises and private people. The rescue and protection work maximizes the cultural value of such ancient books and records. However, after the collection and preservation of ancient books of ethnic minorities, the national wisdom crystallization, which could have been passed down in the folk in active state, can easily become the treasure in the private book cabinets that no one else knows. There are still various kinds of people paying visits to the mountains and villages to search for the small number of ancient books and records of ethnic minorities, some of which have been resold overseas at a profit. Meanwhile, the specific regional conditions for many immovable non-paper ancient books and records are even more regrettable. These stone carvings and cliff engravings bearing ethnic culture are mostly hidden in deep mountains, which are exposed to the weather all the year round. Therefore, the writing symbols or handwriting are so blurred that it is difficult to identify them, or they have directly been damaged by human beings. Natural erosion and gradual disappearance of the stone carvings and cliff engravings is the natural law of development, but it is a huge loss for the ethnic culture.

We have experienced and witnessed several painful moments during the preparation of this series of books. With the support of Yunnan Provincial Department of Finance and Yunnan Provincial Commission of Ethnic and Religious Affairs, we have been consistently pushing forward the project of *Integration of Rare Editions of Ancient Books and Records of Ethnic Minorities in Yunnan*, which is among the one hundred excellent cultural projects in Yunnan Province. Meanwhile, according to the requirements specified in *Notification on the 13th Five-year Plan for the Protection of Ancient Books and Records of Ethnic Minorities issued by National Ethnic Affairs Commission of the People's Republic of China*, "the national census on ancient books of ethnic minorities have been basically completed; the census work has been fully promoted together with relevant departments to find out the resources of ancient books and records of ethnic minorities in various regions. Moreover, the census registration management system shall be established and improved; and a census registration platform shall be constructed to enter, calculate and summarize the census information of ancient books and records of ethnic minorities in various regions, so that the national census registration catalogue of ancient books and records of ethnic minorities can be established." In line with the purpose of "understanding the basic condition and building a platform", we have conducted a general survey and collection of ancient books and records of ethnic minorities in Yunnan Province. For this purpose, we have visited the collection institutions of ancient books and records of ethnic minorities in every prefecture and city of Yunnan Province, and paid visits to the inheritors of ancient books and records and the collectors. Our footprints have almost covered all the regions of Yunnan Province. When we conducted research in Diqing Tibetan Autonomous Prefecture in 2016, the Research Institute of Tibetan Studies in Diqing Tibetan Autonomous Prefecture introduced the preservation and distribution of non-paper ancient books and records in the prefecture, and mentioned that there were many Tibetan stone carvings on the hillside near Tacheng Town of Weixi County. We found the pictures taken by the institute during the field research in the computer several years ago. We could see that half of the hillside was covered with stone carvings, which were all age-old cultural relics. We were so excited. Since there were only a few miles between the distribution location of the stone carvings and Gezi Village where the *Grid Tablet Inscription* engraved in Tibetan language in the Tang Dynasty, and the stone carvings were hidden in the deep mountain, there may be some valuable non-paper ancient records. Unfortunately, we didn't bring the shooting equipment with us, so we decided to go there for investigation later. We didn't expect that we had missed the chance to see its elegant style and features. In May 2018, we organized professional photo-taking, transferring and rubbing personnel to visit Diqing Tibetan Autonomous Prefecture. Led by relevant comrades of Tibetan Institute of Diqing Tibetan Autonomous Prefecture, the group went through the road repair, traffic jam, and hiking in the mountains and came to the hillside tirelessly. However, the scene shocked us, there was no stone carving at all, but a mound mixed with a stone of 5~6 meters in height on the slope. A few Paris polyphylla were planted in the red earth below. After several twists and turns, we got in touch with the comrades of the village committee, and learned that the village had specially assigned bulldozers to level the land so as to develop agricultural economy, and these stone carvings were buried under the mound. This is just a trivial matter we have experienced in the process of the rescue and protection of ancient books and records of ethnic minorities in Yunnan. Such things are happening not only in Diqing, but also in all the regions all over the province. All the stone carvings, cliff engraving, paper literature, silk books, bamboo-slip and wooden engraving are all confronted with such living dilemma. Personnel devoted to the rescue and protection of the ethnic culture felt deeply distressed, but deeply understand that the force of a department and even some groups is so weak to carry out the rescue and protection task. Based on such situation, it is urgent to rescue and protect non-paper ancient books and records. In view of the restriction of funds, personnel, technology and various other aspects, it is suggested that pictures of these culture heritages should be kept for the use of social science research even using the simplest and the most traditional way. Meanwhile, we call on the whole society to attach importance to the rescue and protection of ethnic ancient books and records, which is a profound cause, and also the most actual starting point at the beginning of planning of this series of books.

Yunnan People's Publishing House has offered vigorous supports to the rescue, protection, collation and publication of ancient books and records of ethnic minorities in Yunnan. The project of the rescue and protection of non-paper ancient books and records of ethnic minorities in Yunnan Province was funded by the publication fund for ancient books and records in the ethnic minority languages through application in 2016. Several years ago, Yunnan Provincial Planning Office of Sorting and Publishing Ancient Books of Ethnic Minorities collected ancient books and records from the ethnic minority areas for many times, trying to obtain the clues and take pictures. Yunnan non-paper ancient books and records collected by Lijiang Museum, Lijiang Dongba Culture Research Institute, the Library in Yulong Naxi Autonomous County of Lijiang and Yunnan non-paper ancient books and records collected by folk collectors are finally integrated and published in this book after years of efforts. In order to collect these non-paper ancient books and records, relevant personnel have made great efforts and their footprints almost covered the whole regions of Yunnan Province. After collecting a great deal of original data, we encountered unprecedented difficulties in the classification and integration of the ancient books and records. Carriers of the non-paper ancient books and records in various ethnic minorities can be said to be in a great variety, and the quantity and quality of each carrier type of ancient books and records are at different levels. Since it is taken as the carrier form of a series of books that are summarized and published and comprehensively cover the representative non-paper ancient books and records, it should also take the non-paper ancient books and records covering all the ethnic minorities into account. Not only shall the precious and fine works of non-paper ancient books and records of various ethnic minorities be identified and selected, but also the emotional value of ethnic ancient books in ethnic society shall be taken into consideration as much as possible. The precious ancient books shall be objectively collected and included, and the volume and scale of books shall be also taken into consideration. Through several confirmations, we find that it is almost impossible to classify the non-paper ancient books and records in Yunnan in accordance with the discipline classification of the ethnic ancient books and records. We can only make a general classification of the non-paper ancient books and records that we have collected with all our efforts, and then classify each volume into different subcategories. The rescue and protection of ancient books and records of ethnic minorities is a long-term painstaking task, which cannot be completed in a short period. We were expected to present the high-quality and precious works of Yunnan non-paper ancient books and records comprehensively, but we are constantly discovering new ancient books and records and expanding new categories in our practical work. Therefore, there are inevitably some improper aspects in the series of books, so we can only hope for the forgiveness and corrections of the experts earnestly.

In conclusion, this series of books are the first large-scale integration and collection of non-paper ancient books and records of ethnic minorities in Yunnan. It is for the first time that numerous ancient books and precious records of ethnic minorities, which have been kept secret in the past, are shown to the public. They have been provided with many unique features in terms of academic, historical, inheritance, appreciation and collection value. Moreover, it is of great significance in protecting the cultural heritage of various ethnic minorities, carrying forward their excellent culture, enhancing ethnic unity and promoting the construction of the common spiritual homeland of the Chinese Ethnic Peoples.

目录

云南少数民族非纸质典籍聚珍

YUNNAN SHAOSHU MINZU FEIZHIZHI DIANJI JUZHEN

YUNNAN SHAOSHU MINZU
FEIZHIZHI DIANJI JUZHEN

云南少数民族非纸质典籍聚珍

普米塔朗图

普米塔朗图概述

在遥远的中国西南边陲横断山脉深处，有一片为巍巍山峦、滔滔江水环抱的区域，在这块滇川藏接壤交界的土地上，世世代代生活着一个自称为“普米”（汉文文献称为“西番”或“巴苴”）的山地民族。普米族源自远古时期居住在我国西北河湟谷地的羌人，约在秦汉之际，迁徙游牧至中国西南的大渡河、雅砻江和金沙江流域，并在此世代繁衍生息。据2020年全国第七次人口普查统计，普米族现有45012人（其中，云南省有43061人，约占全国普米族总人口的95%），主要分布在云南省怒江州的兰坪县，丽江市的宁蒗县、玉龙县、永胜县和迪庆州的维西县、香格里拉市，其余散居在昆明市、普洱市、临沧市以及大理州等地。在数千年的历史发展进程中，这个人口不多的山地民族创造了极富特色的物质文明和精神文明。其中，古老的韩规教及其文化构成了普米族精神文化史中最为重要的部分，对普米人和普米族社会以及普米族的民族性、民族精神都产生了非同寻常的影响。

一、普米韩规古籍

普米族有自己的语言，当前学界普遍认为普米语属汉藏语系藏缅语族羌语支，分南北两个方言，南部方言以兰坪、丽江、维西三县交界处的老君山、拉巴山区域为代表，北部方言区主要集中在宁蒗北部永宁、拉伯、翠玉等地区，并与紧邻的四川“西番”（已划为藏族）语属同一方言。[①] 过去，学界认为普米族没有本民族的古老文字，20世纪80年代初，严汝娴等学者调查发现在普米族木垒子的建房木料上，有许多用砍刀、斧头砍制的刻画符号，以及用锅底灰加酒调和而成的墨汁书写的符号，内容包括占有符号、方位符号和数字符号等三类。这些刻划符号是“从结绳记事和刻木记事向图画文字发展的中间环节”，而普米族先民“正是在刻划符号的基础上，开始创造图画文字”。[②] 尔后，严汝娴等学者研究认为：“宁蒗和木里的普米族曾用过简单的图画文字，字数虽少，已堪称萌芽状态的原始文字。”[③] 历史上，普米人中的韩规祭司和皈依藏传佛教的僧侣（喇嘛）直接学习和使用藏文，尤其是历代的韩规们普遍用

① 此观点参见陆绍尊《普米语简志》，民族出版社1983年版；《普米族简史》编写组：《普米族简史》，民族出版社2009年版；等等。但就普米语语支、方言划分、归类等问题目前尚有较大的研究空间。

② 严汝娴：《普米族的刻划符号——兼谈对仰韶文化刻划符号的看法》，载《考古》1982年第3期。

③ 严汝娴、王树五：《普米族简史》，云南人民出版社1988年版，第4页。

古藏文作为书写工具，抄写了大量的苯教经典及谱谍等世俗文书，至今留下了卷帙浩繁的文献，成为中华文化遗产的重要组成部分。

普米韩规古籍的产生、发展与普米族的韩规文化息息相关。原始宗教也被称为“原生性宗教”，国外也有称之为 indigenous religion 的，意思是“本土宗教”“原住民宗教”。从祖国的大西北到大西南，普米先民经历了艰辛的迁徙，在长期与自然抗争和他族的相互适应中建立了自己的世界观，产生了原始宗教——韩规教。因民间把普米族祭司称为“韩规”，故而学术界给普米族的宗教冠名为“韩规教”。“韩规”的本义是“密咒师”“持密咒者”或“密咒之王”，引伸为“智者”，即有智慧的人。韩规在普米族社会中具有很高的社会地位，被视为人与神、鬼之间的媒介，能迎福驱鬼，消除民间灾难，能祈求神灵给人间带来安乐。韩规知识渊博，具备天文、地理、农牧、医药、礼仪等知识，他们是韩规文化的主要继承者和传播人。此外，韩规还是普米族民间绘画艺术家。韩规在做仪式时，要画出各种各样的神灵、人物、动物、植物以及妖魔鬼怪的形象，这种服务于宗教活动的各种绘画，统称为韩规画。时至今日，韩规教保存有完整的仪式系统，以及与各种仪式相配套的古藏文手抄本经典（普米民间称之为“韩规吉吉”，意思是韩规书）。这些散发着松香竹韵、烟渍斑斑的古书，凝聚着普米先民对宇宙、人生的冥想，对天、地、人、神、鬼的理解与诠释，对生、老、病、死的探索，记录了普米人在漫漫岁月中的悲欢离合、世路沧桑。

以塔朗图为代表的绘画类非纸质典籍是普米韩规古籍中最具艺术性、民俗性的文化瑰宝。韩规绘画类古籍按载体可分为木牌画、纸牌画、卷轴画三种，其中木牌画、卷轴画是目前可见最具代表性的普米族非纸质典籍。韩规木牌是祭祀时插立在地上的韩规祭祀用具，也是韩规文化中很古老独特的一种绘画艺术形式。木牌画的内容因韩规作法道场之不同而名目繁多。卷轴画，指以颜料绘制在布质卷轴上的各种神像画（早期以麻布居多，后期的一些用土白布绘制）。普米语谓“舍通”，这些神像轴画，每幅画一主神，周遭绘着与其相关的神界及各种宗教吉祥符号，这些图画多由韩规举行各种仪式时挂在临时设置的神坛上方，表示由它们守护着神坛。卷轴画有长卷、多幅和独幅多种。其内容主要表现古代普米族信仰的神灵鬼怪和各种理想世界，其中也反映了古代普米族社会的各种世俗生活。

二、塔朗图的内容

所谓“塔朗图”，按照普米语来解读，“塔”意为“解脱”，“朗”意为“道路”，全意为“解脱之道”，故也可称之为“解脱之道图”。塔朗图作为一种宗教绘画艺术，一般用于“二次葬”（普米语谓“戎毕”，意为“献祭绵羊”）的超度仪式上。作为丧葬仪式中使用的一种长卷图，其描绘内容大概是，为亡灵排忧解难，把其从鬼界的煎熬中解脱超度出来，在人类之地转生为人，或送至神灵之地。

塔朗图全卷以分段连续的形式，勾线填色的表现手法完成。全图内容分为三部分，分别为鬼界（包括“地狱道”“饿鬼之地”和“畜牲之地”）、人界（“人间之地”）、天界（“神灵世界”）。鬼界描述了人在生前有过不规范行为或杀生等行为，死后会经过“尼瓦”（地狱），并受到阴间阎罗王（尼瓦启级甲布）、地狱判官和狱卒的阻拦，且阐述了不同的亡魂根据生前所犯的罪行，分别受到相应的惩罚。人界则是一个中间地段，是一个沟通和连接着地狱与天堂的地带。人界中充满着温馨，图中描绘人间的美丽景象：一颗神树（普米语谓“巴松炯使崩”，传说这棵神树维系着人类的生命，故亦称之为“生命树”）， 树上栖息着一只神鸟，普米语谓“甲依穷迁隔布”，其形为鹰嘴、龙角、人身、鹰爪，张开着翅膀，身穿虎皮裤、嘴里含着蛇（孽龙）；神树周遭绘着与其相关的飞禽走兽，如狮、龙、虎、豹、獐子、山鹿、野兔、老鹰、羊(山羊、绵羊)、牛、马及大象等；顶部左右两端所绘的是日、月；底部则绘有“尔罗莲布”（湖海）及所产之宝物——鱼、白海螺等，一派吉祥的景象呈现在眼前，仿佛是人间福音，又是神界祥瑞。天界即神界（普米语称之为“亨甸”，意为“神之领域”），一个美好的世界，即极乐世界。在神界，通常绘有十三层天界的诸神、吉祥花和一些教符等。

三、塔朗图的艺术和文化特征

塔朗图呈现出一种原始的自然美，是普米族绘画中别具一格的艺术珍品。其艺术特色首先体现在鬼神的造型上，人身兽首、龇牙咧嘴、造型奇特、形态生动，尤其对堕入地狱的亡灵进行各种各样的惩罚，使人观之触目惊心，心有余悸，发挥了通过生命礼仪教化社群德行的作用。画者用极其简练的笔法，运用夸张的造型手段，描绘形象奇异诡谲、拙朴而充满稚趣。在色彩的运用上，采用明度较暗的颜色，如黑色、蓝色、青色、墨绿。譬如说，描绘地狱道里的黑色的铁三角、墨绿的鼎炉、黑山、黑头鬼等，整个色调灰黑，表现出阴森、恐怖、想象中的地狱之状。在构图形式上也是采取了多种表现手法，如运用了均衡对称的构图形式，丰富简练的造型，敷色多以红、绿、黄、白、蓝，对比强烈，色彩艳丽，富有强烈的装饰性形式美感，表示出人们对美好生活的向往。

其次，我们在塔朗图中看到多种宗教文化融合的特点，反映了普米人多元文化相融而成的灵魂观和生命观。如鬼狱所描绘的惩罚亡灵之刑，既有普米族多元的传统伦理思想和民间习俗的反映，又与藏传佛教《六道轮回图》所描述的内容有诸多相似之处。有的内容如为死者亡灵而设的地狱黑锅，普米语谓“尼瓦让”， 锅圈内有三种畜牲：鸽、蛇、猪，且三种动物互咬联成一环（猪咬蛇尾，蛇咬鸽尾，鸽又咬着猪的尾巴）。从佛学的角度来讲，这三种动物，分别表义贪、嗔、痴三毒。此外，十三层天界的诸神或菩萨，36朵吉祥花以及点缀在这些吉祥花上的本教教符“卍”等，都与藏族的本教和藏传佛教有密切的渊源关系。

无疑，韩规教接受了佛教“三界六道”说的一些观念，产生了描述生命历程的鸿篇巨制塔朗图，并把它运用于丧葬超度仪式。但有意思的是，这种佛教观念并未能取代本民族传统的生命归宿观，而是形成了一种传统与外来文化因素并存于丧葬文化中的现象。一方面，韩规在丧仪上铺开塔朗图，咏诵有关地狱、人间、天堂的经书，为死者超度灵魂，帮助死者转生于人间和神界；另一方面，又咏诵描述传统送魂路线的韩规经，把死者灵魂送往祖居之地，而且确切地指示亡灵必经的具体路站名。在普米人心目中，回归祖居之地是根深蒂固的观念，即使韩规依塔朗图把亡灵超度往神地，人们还是认为死者实际上是沿着韩规经所指引的送魂路线回到祖地去了。显然，在塔朗图中可见多种宗教文化的融合，包括藏传佛教、本教和印度婆罗门教等，反映了普米族多元文化相融而成的生命与灵魂观，反映了各民族之间的交往、交流和交融。

本书收录的普米韩规塔朗图共有三个版本：一是丽江市许正强、兰碧瑛夫妇所收藏的塔朗图，绘在纸张上，再粘贴于经过上浆处理的蓝色棉布上，年代为清代，尽管有些画面边缘破损，但大体保存完好，且构图精密严谨，人物造型生动。二是丽江市博物院所藏的塔朗图，绘在经过上浆处理的蓝色棉布上，年代较早，虽画面有些模糊，但品相完整。三是宁蒗县新营盘乡东风村马金荣家收藏的塔朗图，绘在经过上浆处理的土白布上，年代较晚，虽系临摹之作，但画面清晰，色彩鲜艳。可以说，它们是难得一见的普米族非纸质典籍珍品，融汇了多种民族文化因素的古籍实物，对于研究普米族的宗教、历史、艺术、民俗等具有重要的价值。

塔朗图（一）①

塔朗图（一）
尺寸：长 705 厘米，宽 23 厘米
收藏单位：丽江市博物院

① 普米塔朗图、纳西东巴神路图依据使用仪规，细节图从地狱部分排起。文物标签系文物征集入库时粘贴的标签，因古籍上有藏文，故命名为“藏文神路图”，经专家鉴定、识别，确定为普米塔朗图。特此说明。

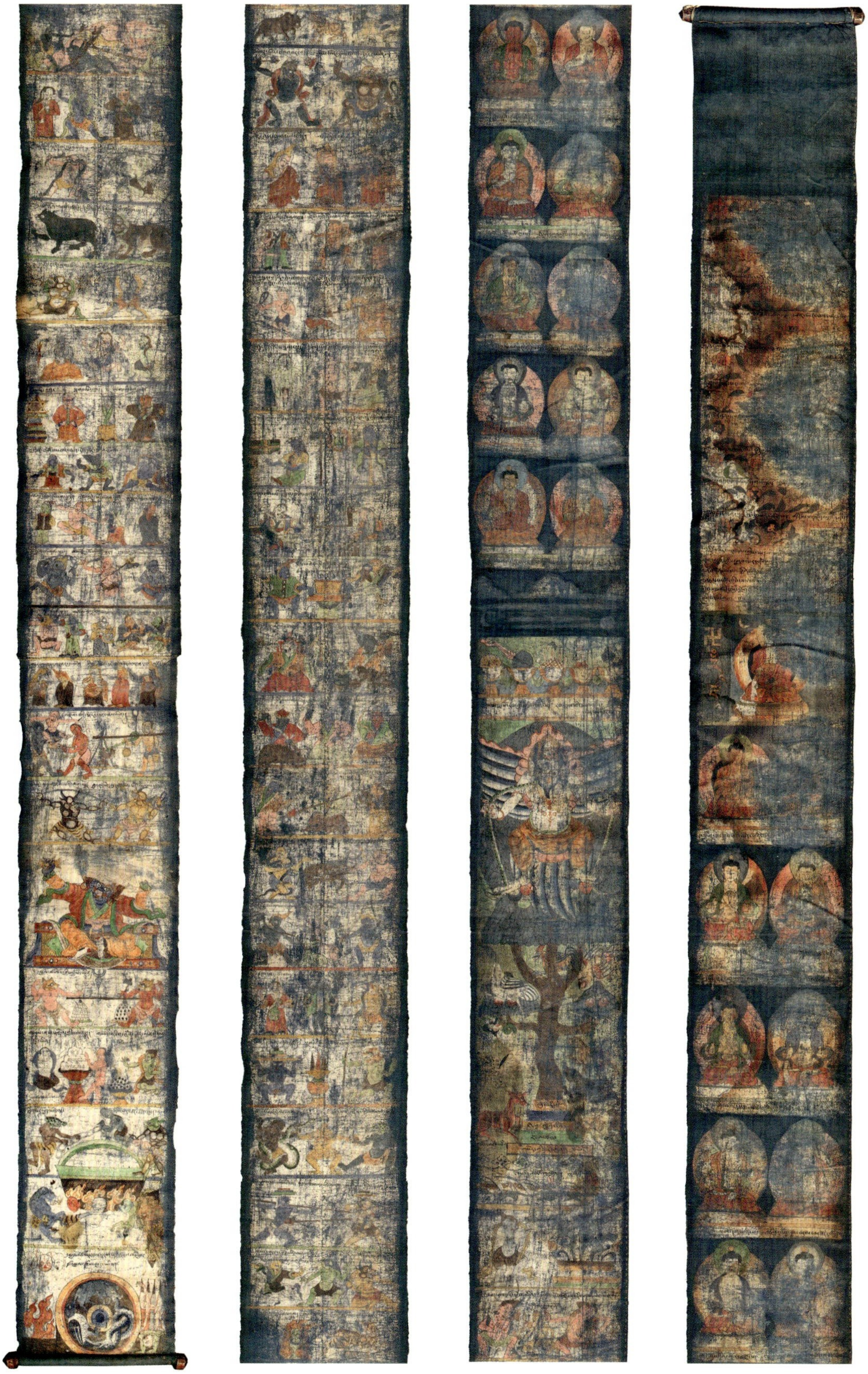

普米塔朗图

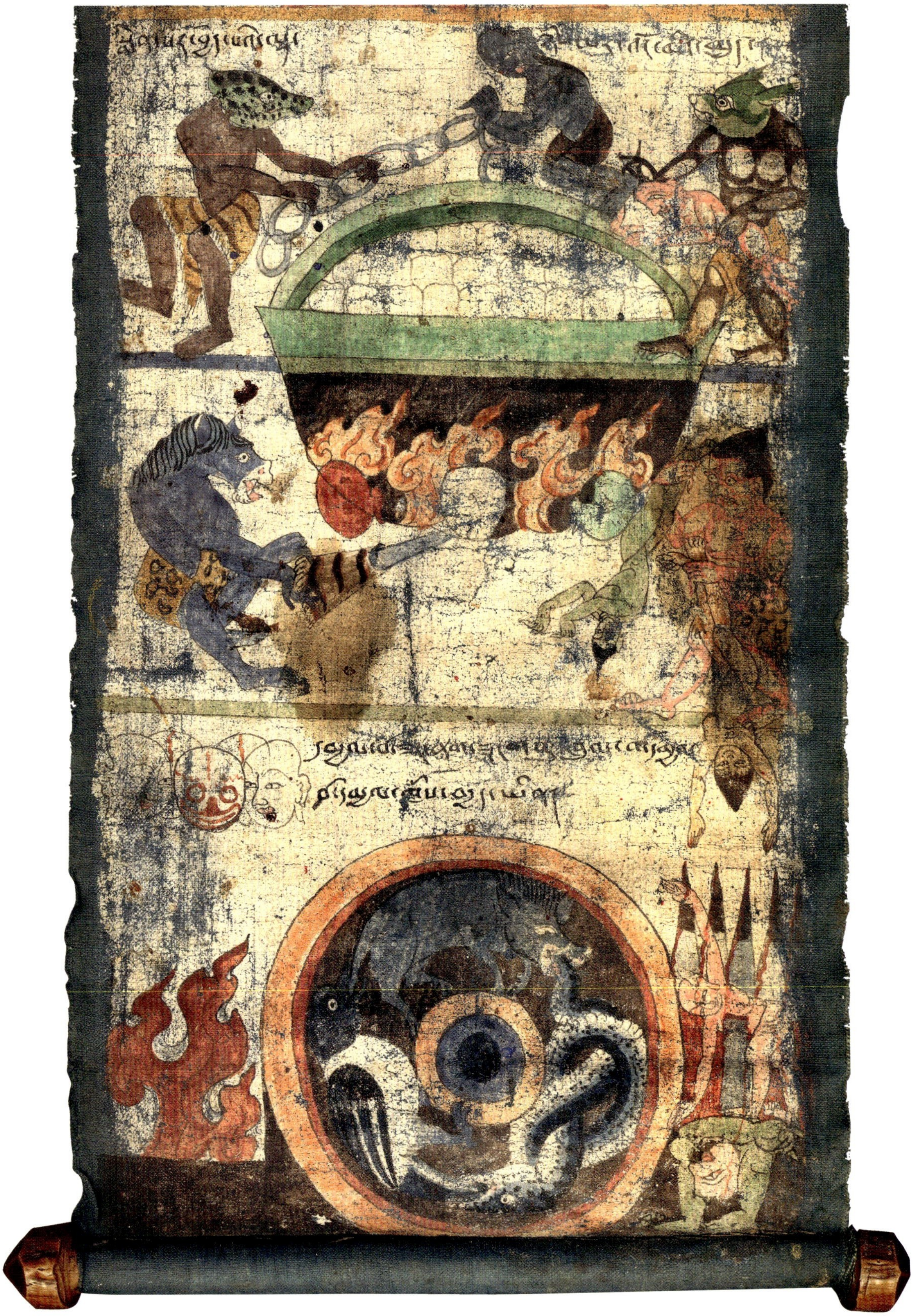

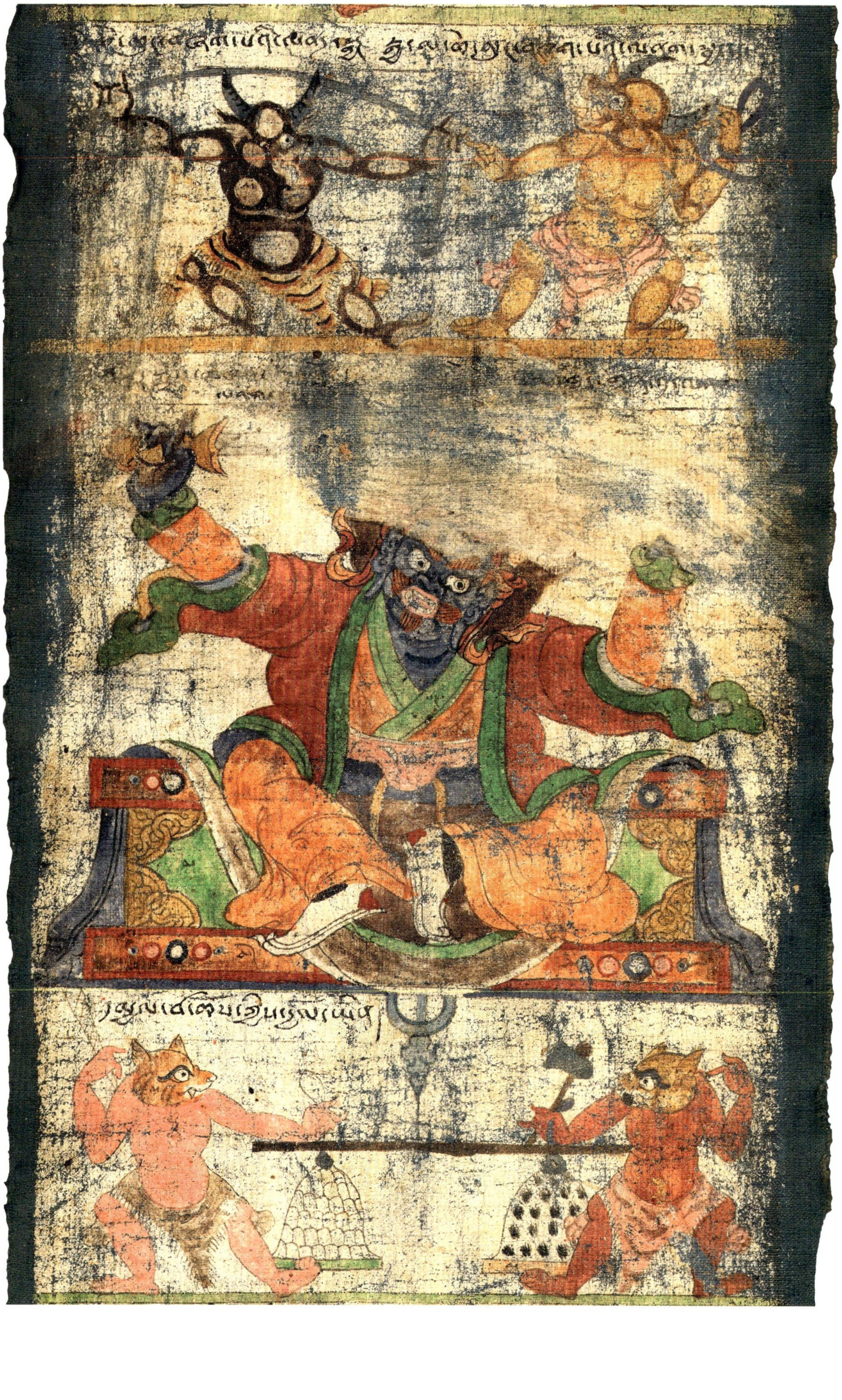

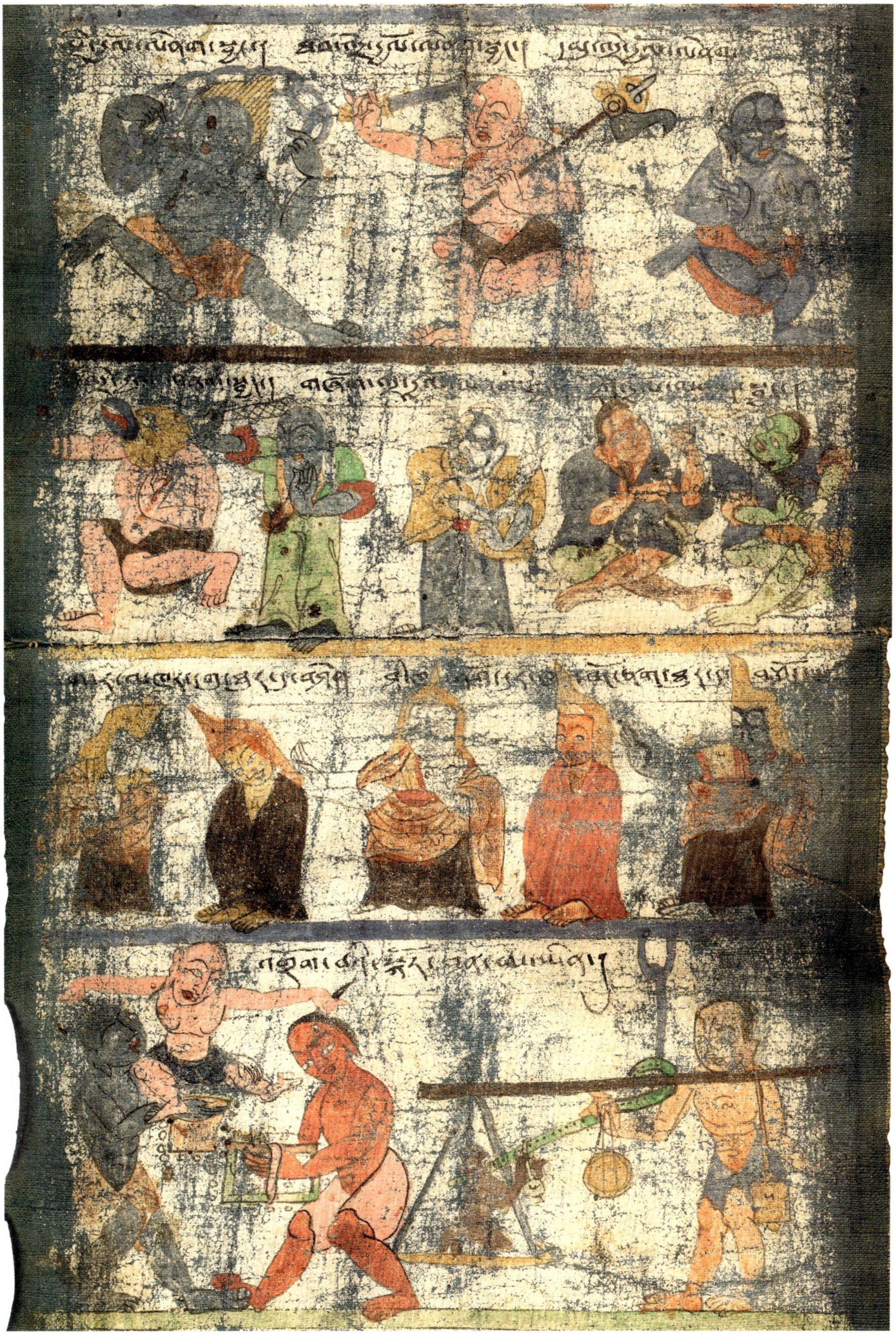

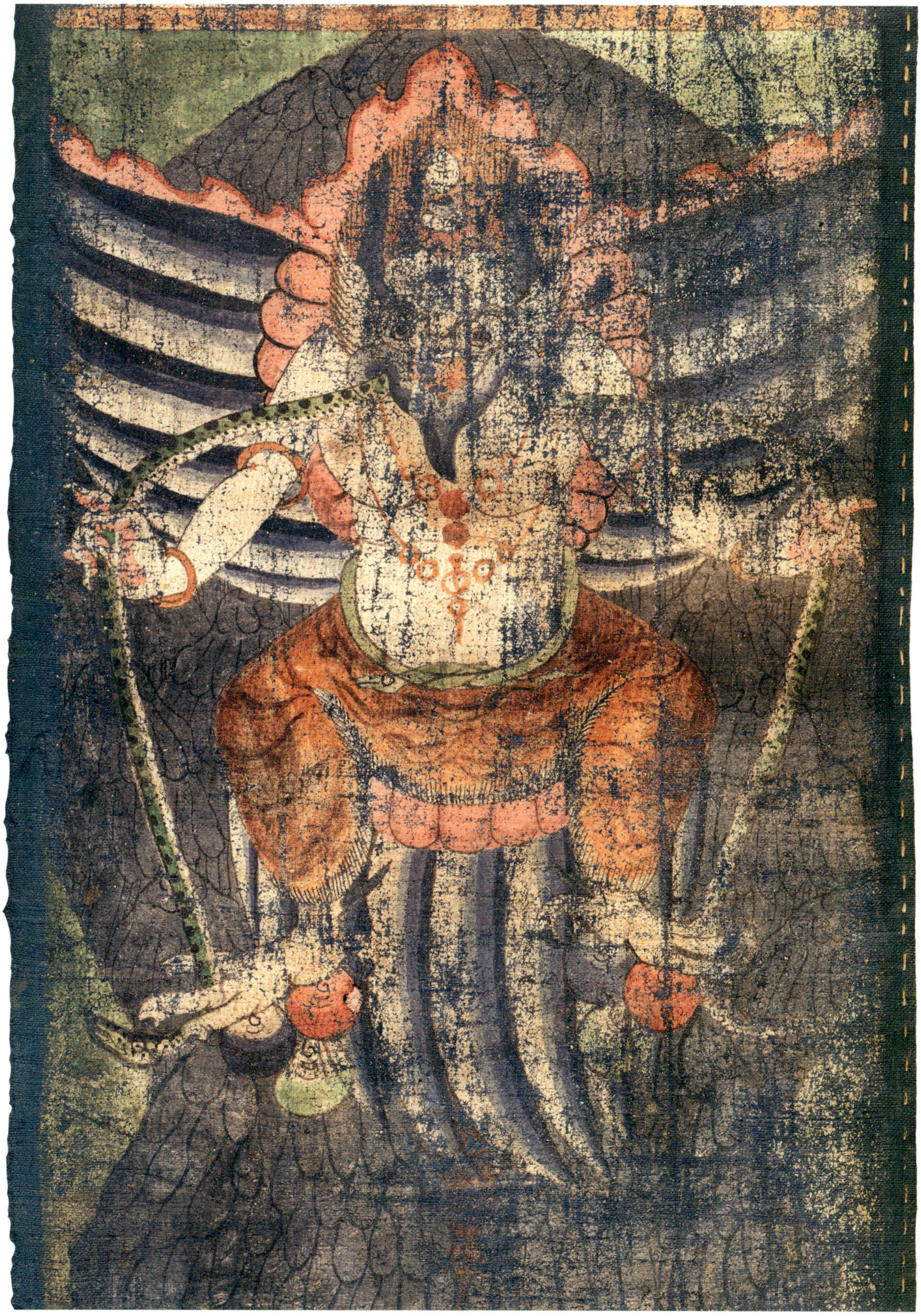

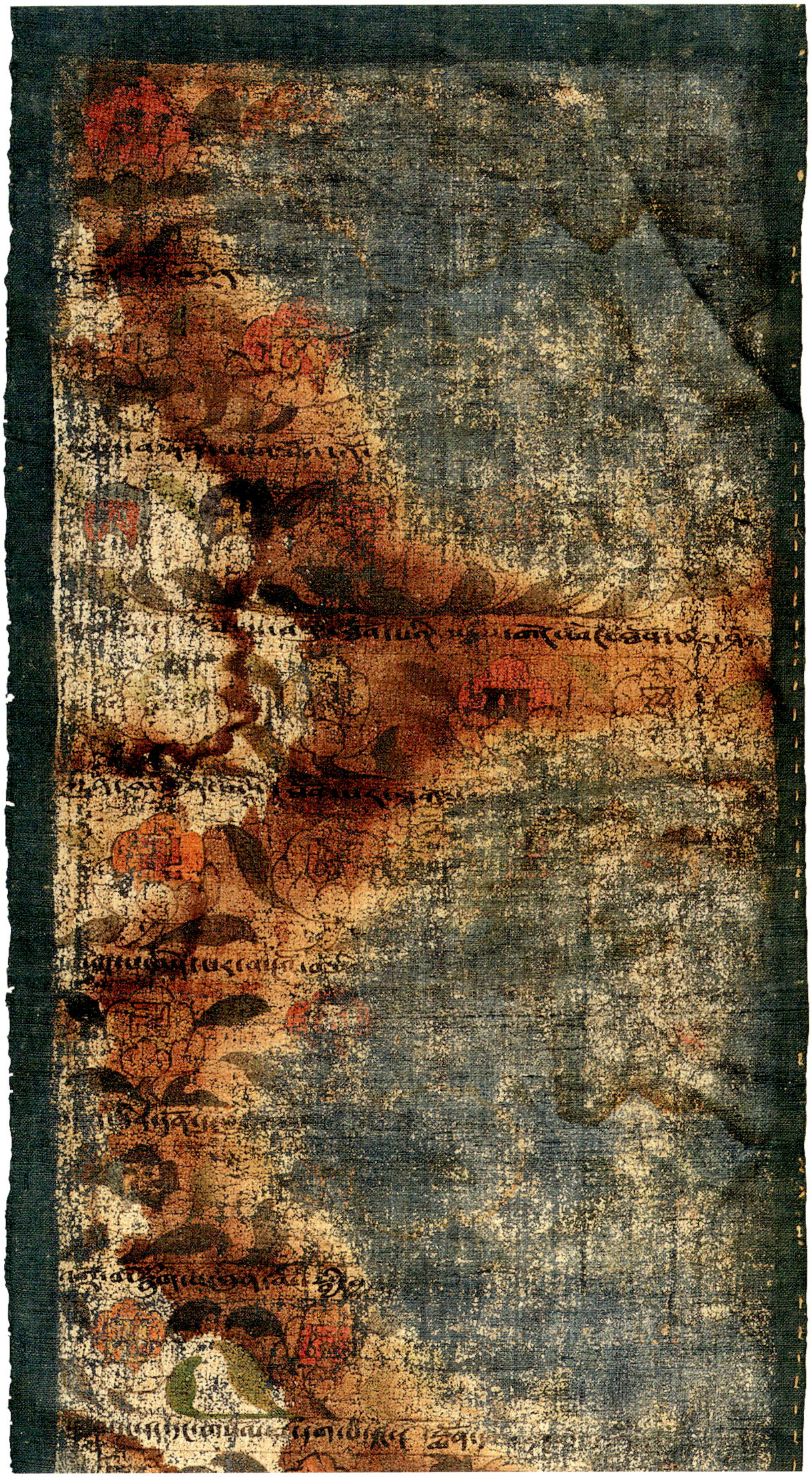

塔朗图（二）

塔朗图（二）
尺寸：长540厘米，宽18厘米
供图：许正强、兰碧瑛

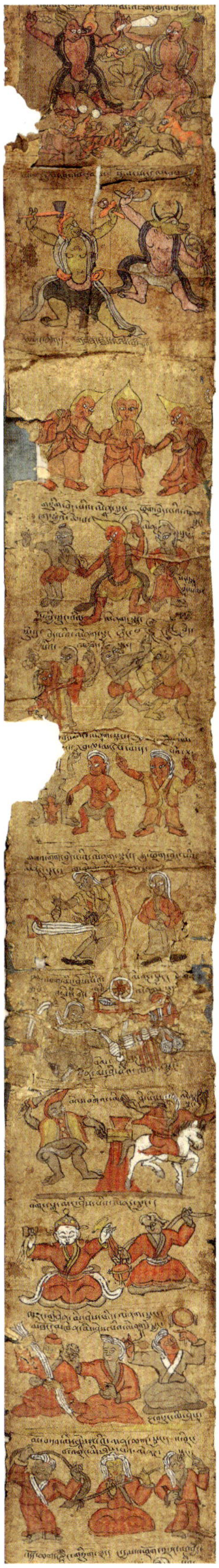

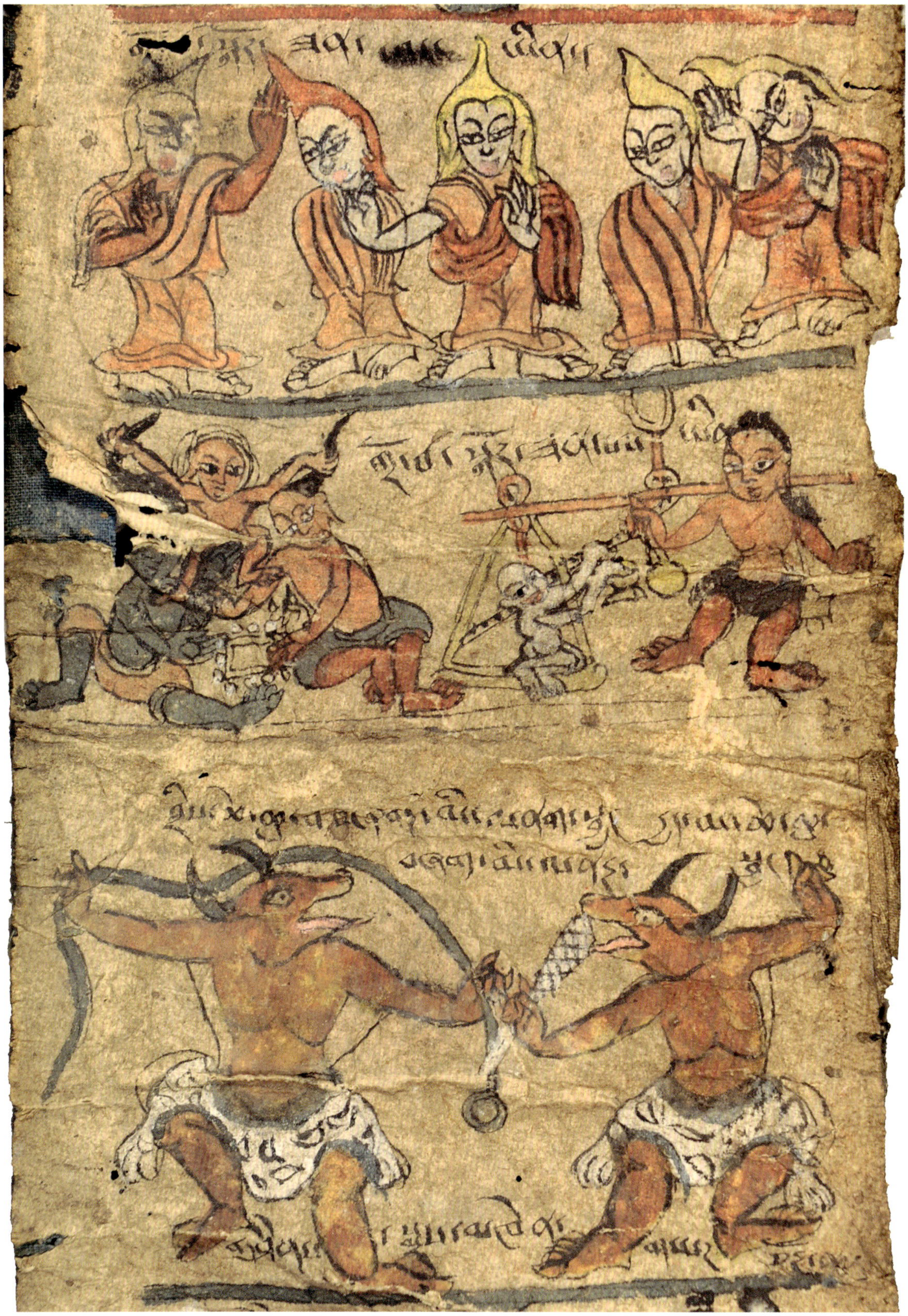

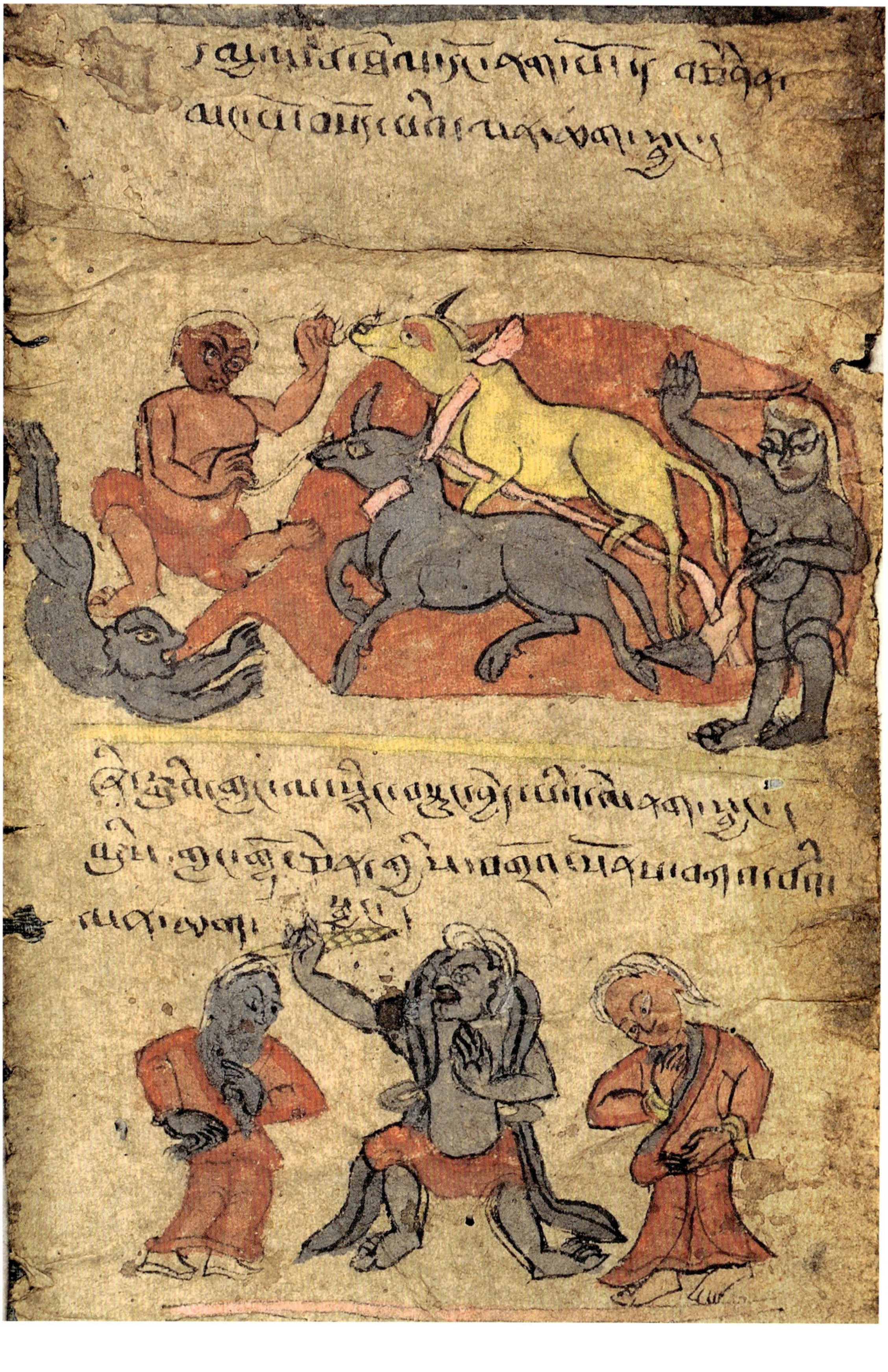

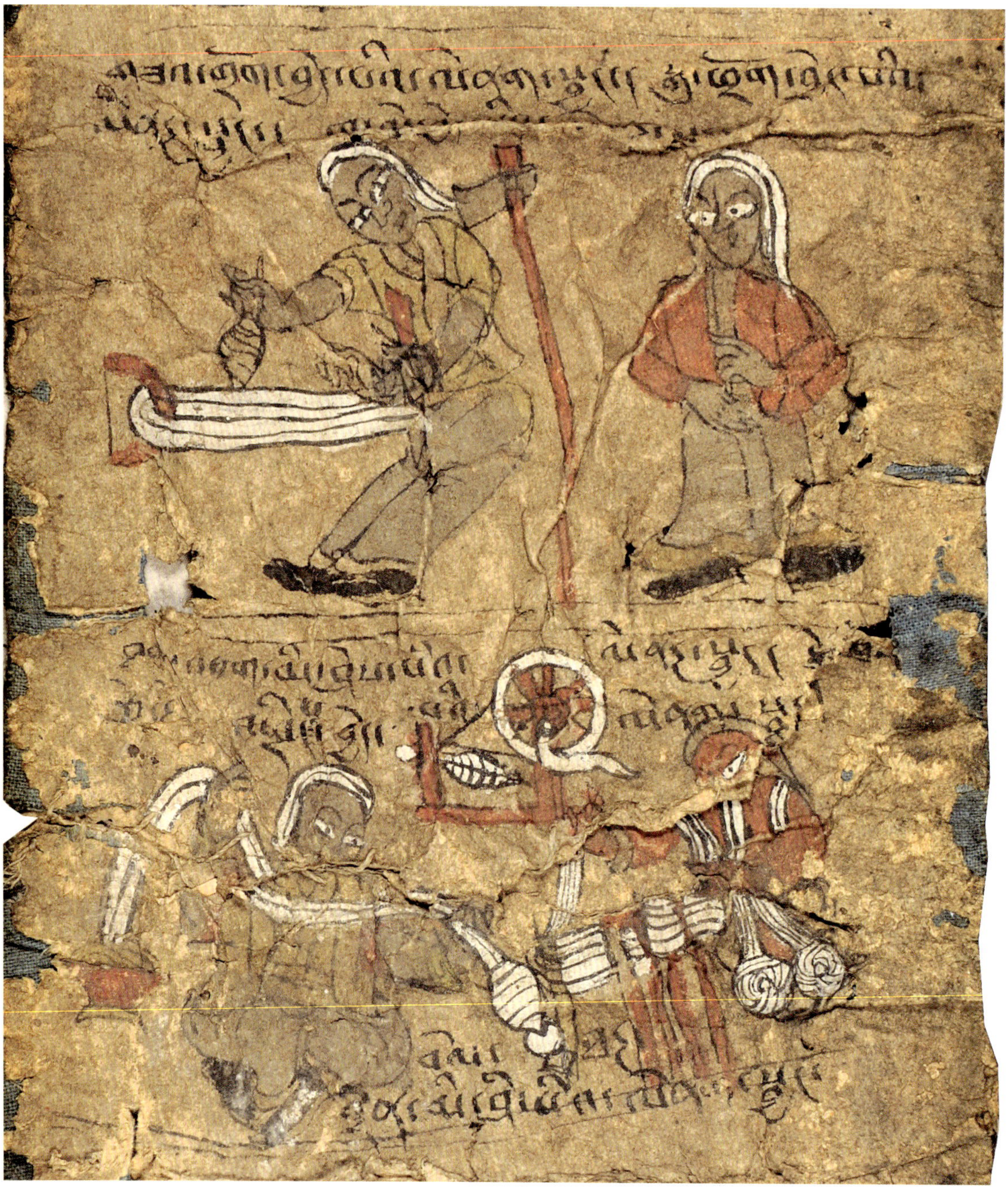

塔朗图（三）

塔朗图（三）
尺寸：长 800 厘米，宽 30 厘米
供图：胡文明

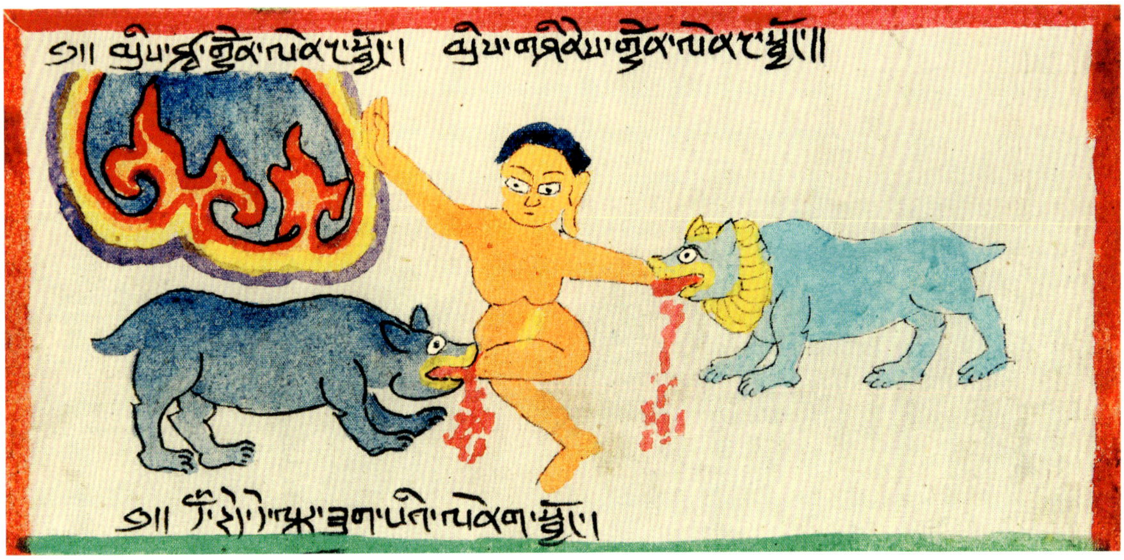

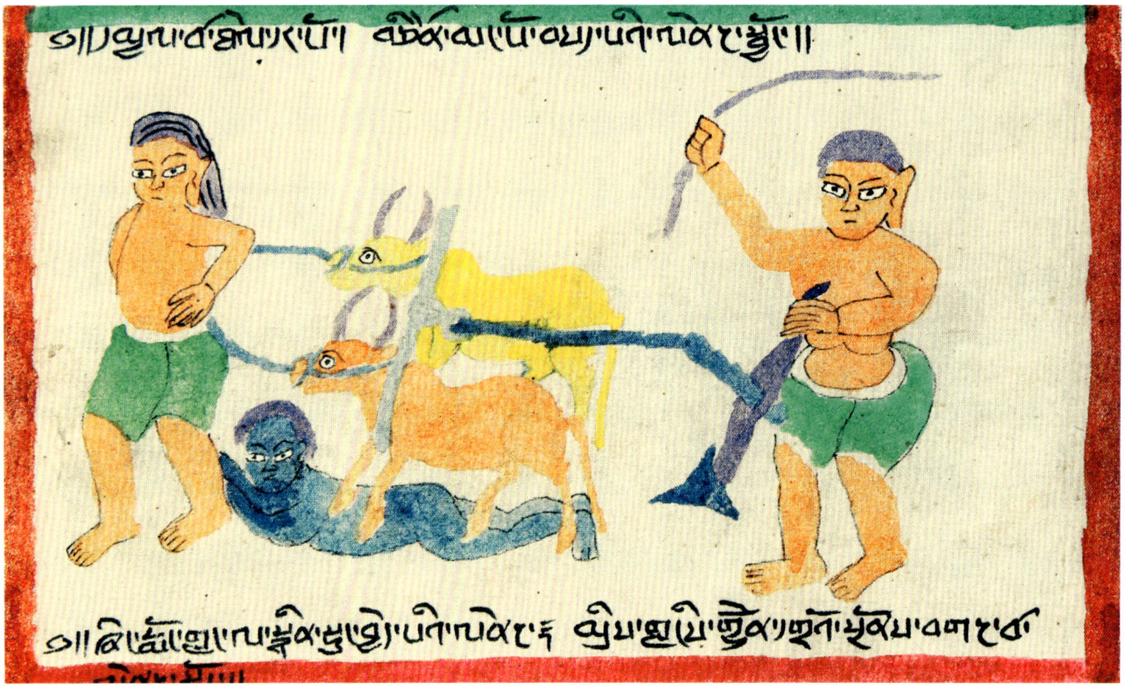

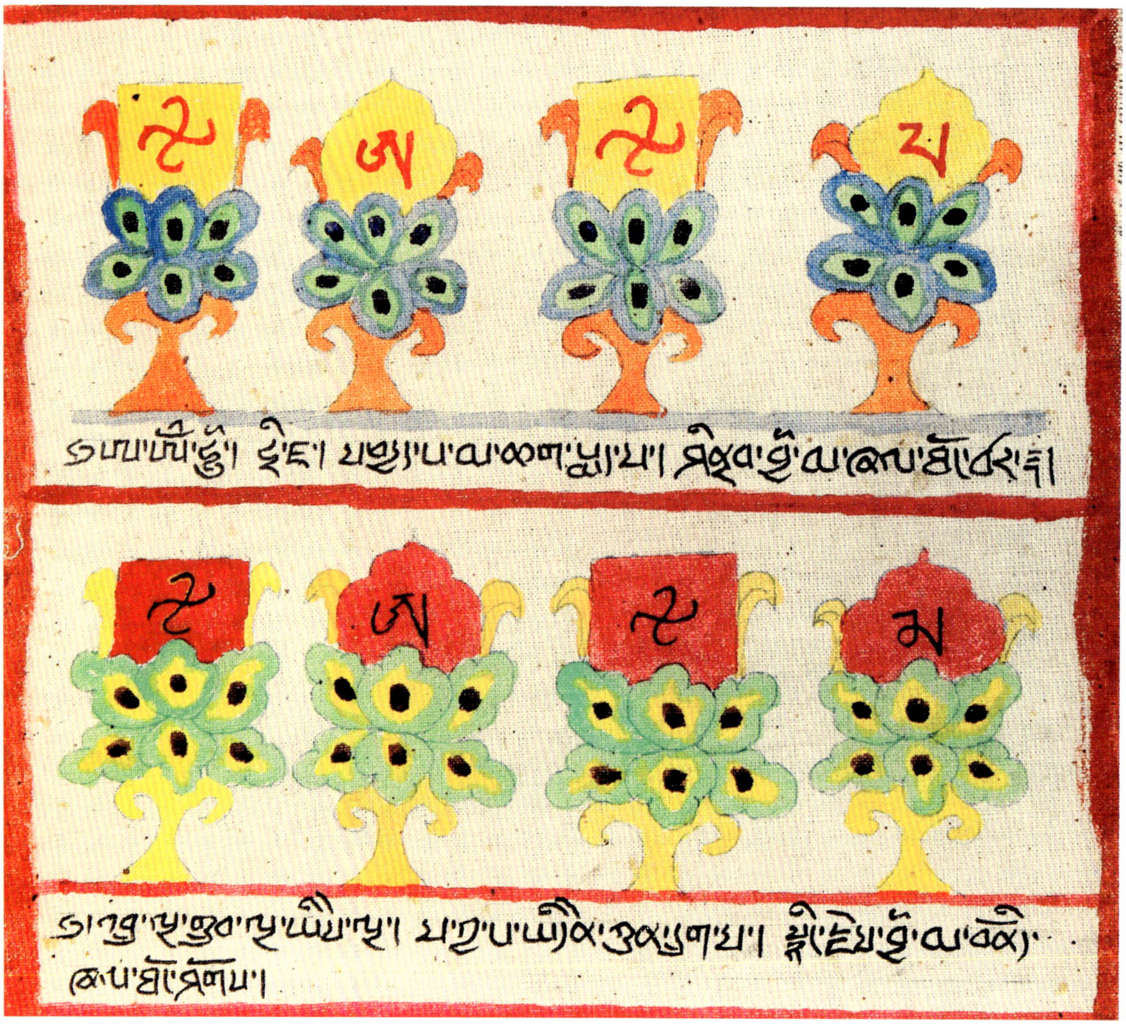

YUNNAN SHAOSHU MINZU
FEIZHIZHI DIANJI JUZHEN

云南少数民族非纸质典籍聚珍

纳西东巴神路图

纳西东巴神路图概述

纳西族是云南世居少数民族之一，拥有悠久的历史和深厚的文化，近代以来主要聚居于金沙江上游地带的云南省丽江市古城区、玉龙纳西族自治县、宁蒗彝族自治县、永胜县，迪庆藏族自治州香格里拉市、维西傈僳族自治县、德钦县，怒江傈僳族自治州贡山独龙族怒族自治县，四川省凉山彝族自治州盐源县、木里藏族自治县，攀枝花市盐边县、甘孜藏族自治州巴塘县和西藏自治区芒康县等地。自称“纳（naq）”“纳西（Naqxi）”“纳日（Naqssee）”“纳恒”（Naqhal）等，历代史籍中有“摩沙夷”“磨些蛮”“末些”“摩娑”“麽些”“摩”“摩荻”“么”“摩梭”等称谓。1956 年，统一族名为“纳西”。据相关学者研究，纳西族与远古时期分布在我国西北河湟地带的古羌人有渊源关系，据《后汉书·西羌传》《华阳国志》《蜀中广记》等推断，纳西族先民自河湟地带“向南迁徙至岷江上游，又西南至雅砻江流域，又西迁至金沙江上游东西地带”[①]，唐初已广泛分布于今滇藏川毗连区的广大区域。唐代初期以前，纳西族分布区以今盐源一带为中心。唐初到元初，纳西族分布中心区从盐源拓展至今天的丽江诸地。元明以来，以丽江诸地为中心的纳西族地区社会经济有了极大发展。清初的改土归流进一步促进了区域民族融合，纳西族融于其他民族，汉族及其他少数民族亦有融入纳西族者。据 2020 年第七次全国人口普查统计，截至 2020 年 11 月 1 日零时纳西族有人口 323767 人。[②]

一、纳西非纸质典籍及其种类

纳西族古籍是纳西族传统文化的重要载体，包括用纳西族文字及汉文书写的、反映纳西族历史文化的手稿、经卷、典籍、文献、谱牒、楹联、铭刻、文书，以及

① 方国瑜、和志武：《纳西族的渊源、迁徙和分布》，载《民族研究》1979 年第 1 期，第 33–41 页。
② 国务院第七次全国人口普查领导小组办公室编：《中国人口普查年鉴（2020）》，中国统计出版社 2022 年版。

神话传说、史诗歌谣、民间故事等口传古籍，其中用纳西族文字创作、传世的古籍最具代表性。纳西族历史上创制过东巴文（含阮可文、玛丽玛莎文）和哥巴文两种文字系统，其中用东巴文撰写的存世古籍有1000多种3万余册，亦有少量用哥巴文书写的古籍。东巴文和哥巴文都是一种“宗教经典用字”[①]，主要由东巴教祭司东巴传承，用于书写宗教经典，也有部分东巴或掌握东巴文的群众用以书写医书、谱牒、契约、书信、账目、文书等，传世纳西东巴古籍中，东巴教经籍占绝对比重，应用性文献储量不多。按其内容可将纳西东巴古籍分为五大类：（1）祈福延寿类，包括祭天、祭署、祭祖、祭家神、祭胜利神、祭畜神、祭谷神等。（2）禳鬼消灾类，主要包括抵御灾害、调解矛盾、除秽、驱除瘟疫和厄运等内容。（3）丧葬超度类，包括开丧和超度、超度东巴什罗、超度拉姆、祭凶死鬼、大祭风等。（4）占卜类，有石卜、星卜、梦卜、贝卜、巴格卜等，内容涉及婚丧嫁娶、起房盖屋、生老病死、天象变化等等，如《看日子卜书》《用巴格图占卜》《占梦之书》等。（5）杂类，内容涉及舞蹈、医药、民歌、农桑、工艺等，如《东巴舞谱》《医药之书》《民歌范本》等。

数以万计的东巴古籍，是纳西先民集体智慧和哲学思考之结晶，涉及宗教、历史、语言文字、文学艺术、政治哲学、天文历法、经济、医药、社会生活等诸多方面的内容，被誉为“纳西族古代社会的百科全书”。杨福泉教授在其论著《东巴教通论》一书中充满诗意地说：“在这些散发着松香竹韵的烟渍斑斑的古书中，凝聚着纳西先民对宇宙人生的冥想苦思，对天地人神鬼之秘、万事万物的起源等充满天籁之趣又不乏理性的解释，对人与自然之关系的睿智思考，对天体地理、生老病死的初步探索，记录了纳西人在漫漫岁月中的悲欢离合、世路沧桑。”[②]

纳西东巴古籍中有一批载体多样、形态各异、内容丰富的非纸质典籍。目前所见的纳西族非纸质典籍大体包括以下三类。一是铭刻。包括金石铭刻和竹木铭刻，东巴文铭刻存世者较少。1934年，我国著名历史学家方国瑜曾在丽江金沙江边的桥头危桥下目睹距今约400年的明代哥巴文石刻，刻文大概为“长命永禄”的祈祷词，

① 喻遂生、杨亦花等：《俄亚、白地东巴文化调查研究》，中国社会科学出版社2016年版，第13页。

② 杨福泉：《东巴教通论》，中华书局2012年版，第454页。

遗憾的是此石刻在1951年修路时被毁。据我们所知，丽江市玉龙纳西族自治县宝山乡、塔城乡，四川省凉山彝族自治州木里藏族自治县俄亚纳西族乡存有少量东巴文砖刻、墓碑，如俄亚纳西族汝卡支系在举行竖送魂经幡仪式时需要在玛尼堆旁竖一块东巴文石碑，部分人家还会在家门口、畜圈门口摆放一些具有驱鬼镇邪、祈福禳灾作用的东巴文辟邪石刻；丽江市博物院收藏有一批珍贵的东巴文字砖，东巴文、哥巴文对照印刷雕版等。二是纳西东巴木牌画。木牌画，纳西语称"课标"，指为举行一定的祭祀仪式，用符号和图像在木牌上作画，是一种历史悠久的原始绘画艺术，是东巴艺术萌芽阶段的产物。《云南少数民族非纸质典籍聚珍·竹木简牍类一》收录了丽江市博物馆珍藏的一批珍贵的纳西东巴木牌画。三是卷轴画。纳西语叫"普劳幛"，是东巴用矿物质颜料绘制于土布上的神像画，存世精品众多，有长卷、多幅和独幅等多种，是东巴绘画艺术跨入发达阶段而趋于精熟的标志。独幅卷轴画主要画一尊大神或护法神，大神画有萨依威德、依古阿格、恒迪窝盘和祖师东巴什罗、药神、战神等东巴教神灵体系中的尊神，每幅卷轴画表现某个神祇及其所居的神界。国家图书馆、南京图书馆、中央民族大学、云南省少数民族古籍整理出版规划办公室、丽江东巴文化研究院、丽江市博物院、丽江玉龙纳西族自治县图书馆等机构收藏了数量不等的纳西东巴卷轴画。新近出版的《云南少数民族非纸质典籍聚珍·丝帛素书类一》《云南少数民族古籍珍本集成》《云南少数民族绘画典籍集成》《云南少数民族传统绘画》等图书以彩色影印的方式收录了一批卷轴画珍品。

二、纳西东巴神路图的内容及使用[①]

神路图是东巴卷轴画中最原始、最有代表性的巨作，是纳西族东巴教用于丧葬仪式和超度亡灵仪式上的一种长卷绘画。"亨日皮"其意即为祭司东巴为逝者评断、指引通往神地的"道路"，引导亡灵从鬼地（地狱）的煎熬中解脱出来，在人间转

① 此部分撰写参考李锡主编：《近神之路——纳西族东巴神路图》，云南美术出版社2001年版；杨福泉：《从〈神路图〉看藏文化对纳西族东巴教的影响》，载《云南社会科学》2001年第5期；木仕华：《纳西东巴教神路图中33首大象源流考》，载《西藏民族大学学报（哲学社会科学版）》2017年第9期。

生为人或送至神地的漫长超度之路。

神路图分段连续描绘地狱、人间、天堂三个部分，依次描绘冥界中亡灵要通过的区域。第一个区域——九座黑山，东巴教认为人在世时有不规范的行为或杀生，死后经过这一区域，会遇到各种粗野、凶横的“冷臭”鬼的阻拦。接着通往“尼瓦”地、“依道”地，东巴教中已有人死转世的观念，认为生前有杀生、通奸杀夫、偷盗赌博、谗言害人、玷污同宗女性、经商缺斤少两、放火烧山、污染水源等有违道德人伦、言行不端的，死后可能会在“尼瓦”地、“依道”地中转生。东巴要帮助亡灵通过这些鬼地，从地狱鬼王史支那儿把亡魂赎出来，到达一片吉祥景象的“本慈汝堆”，意即“人类之地”，历经艰辛的亡灵在五行方城转生为人。最终，打开通往神界的大门，进入有着七座神山、七个神湖的神居地，把亡灵送到“三十三个神地”。在一条宽约16—30厘米、长约15米的长条麻布之上，东巴们用色彩饱满的矿物颜料，朴拙、工整的构图手法，完整呈现了超度亡灵的漫长道路。画作上绘有360多个人、神、鬼及70多种奇禽怪兽，被称为我国美术史上最长的直幅长卷，享有“古代宗教绘画第一长卷”之誉。纳西族传统的生命观、伦理观、地域观、死亡观等观念，亦在简朴的笔触间跃然纸上。

人类在度过生命中的重要关口，比如出生、青春期、结婚、为人父母、登科及第、提拔升迁以及死亡时，要举行一系列的生命礼仪，强化群体纽带和度过“危机”。[①]纳西族在面对个体生命的终极危机和整个群体的危机时，通过葬礼这个强化仪式，由东巴根据“神路图”引导死者灵魂进入新的生命空间，同时完成族群、社群的社会调适，缓解因死亡引起的恐惧、不安，使被扰乱的关系恢复到正常的平衡状态。仪式中，祭司铺开神路图，众东巴依规立于图旁，依次吟诵《神路图经》，为死者评断、指引通往神地的路径，引导亡灵摆脱地狱恶鬼的纠缠折磨，逐层向上超度，在人间转生为人，或最终送至神界。其间，东巴还要依据《磋模》跳神舞和动物舞等仪式舞蹈。神路图使用仪轨随着纳西族丧葬制度的变化发生了一些演变，过去实行火葬习俗时，要在火葬场铺开神路图，从死者的头部位置朝东北方向延伸铺开。“改土归流”后，纳西族葬制改为土葬，神路图改为由棺材头部向东北方向延伸铺开。

---

① （美）威廉·A. 哈维兰著，瞿铁鹏、张钰译：《文化人类学》，上海社会科学院出版社2006年版，第374页。

三、纳西东巴神路图的文化内涵及价值

纳西族自唐初以来集中分布于中国西南地区的滇藏川毗连区，汉族、纳西族、藏族、白族、傈僳族、彝族、普米族、怒族等多个民族在此区域共生发展，不同历史时期的民族人口迁移、族际经济往来、族际通婚和多元宗教的传播与扩散等都积极推动了多民族广泛而深入的文化接触与交流。①在这个多元共生的文化场域中产生的纳西东巴神路图，混融了多种宗教文化，特别是本教、佛教的文化内涵，是各民族交往交流交融的有力见证。

纳西东巴神路图文化内涵丰富，其中所蕴含的地狱观、伦理观、生命观等文化观念和文化表达手法，系纳西族基于本民族的原生认知，融儒、释、道、印度教、本教等多元文化创作而成，凸显多元性和文化混融性，下面择一二概述如下：其一，神路图反映的生命观、灵魂观是受佛教“三界六道”论、生死轮回、因果报应等观念影响的产物。如东巴教认为现世生命结束后，可能在“尼瓦六地”转生，在丧葬仪式上，吟诵完《神路图经》后，还要吟诵《尼瓦六地》。这一观念显然是受佛教“五趣六道”说的影响，佛教认为众生根据生前行为，有在地狱、饿鬼、畜生、人、天和阿修罗六道转生的趋向。神路图中描述的有七座神山、七个神湖的神界，亦与佛教神话中描述的须弥山周围有七个香海、七座金山的提法相吻合。超度亡灵的完美归宿——三十三个神地，则与《大智度论》卷九描述的“须弥山高八万四千由旬，上有三十三天城”②有相似之处，杨福泉教授认为“纳西族关于三十三个神地的观念是受印度文化的影响，可能是通过藏传佛教传入东巴教中”③。其二，神路图受藏文化，特别是本教文化和藏传佛教的影响深远。如，神路图描述亡灵历经鬼地的千般苦楚后，到达绘有十三盏酥油灯、十三个月亮、十三个神石、十三个“多玛”、十三棵刺柏树、十三朵花、十三只鸟的人类之地，人间诸事物皆为“十三”是源于

① 王丽萍、周智生：《滇藏川毗连地区族际文化互动的空间特性研究》，载《西南民族大学学报（人文社会科学版）》2017年第8期。

② 释明贤：《三宝论·法宝论》，宗教文化出版社2014年版，第148页。

③ 杨福泉：《从〈神路图〉看藏文化对纳西族东巴教的影响》，载《云南社会科学》2001年第5期。

本教的数字崇拜[①]。此外，神路图所描述的亡灵在五方城转生，在东方，人从白色的蛋里出生；在南方，人由女性孕育；在西方，神从花中诞生；在北方，神从树上诞生，这段内容与《西藏度亡经》所述卵生、胎生、化生和湿生四种转生方式相似。其三，神路图吸收、融汇了具有汉文化特色的伦理观。如神路图描绘的鬼界和惩戒罪人的诸种罪孽，与《玉历宝钞劝世文》《玉历钞传警世》等书中阐述的相关内容有着异曲同工之效，与藏族《格萨尔王传》中描述的 24 个惩罚之域，与佛教的“十恶”都有共同之处，由此折射出中华民族历来是一个崇善的民族，向往善、追求善、成就善，要求每一个社会成员都要存善心、讲善言、行善事，方能得善终。

纳西东巴神路图既是融汇多元文化的文化精品，又是纳西族传统文化艺术中的杰出作品，其文化和艺术价值不言而喻。本书精选丽江市博物院珍藏的 3 幅神路图，并将其与普米族塔朗图编排在一册，作引玉之砖，以期民族学、民族史、民族艺术等相关学科作更深入的研究。

① 此观点参见卡尔梅《本教历史及教义概述》，见中央民族学院藏族研究所《藏族研究译文集》第 1 辑，1983 年，第 64–77 页。

Naqxi dobbaq heiqreepiq ko sel

Naqxi ceef chee Yuiqnaiq zzeeq gge sasvl miqcvf ddeehual waq, liqshee sherq ssua, veiqhual goqwa yi ssua, jildail ddeeggaiq seil Yibbiq ggeqzul gge Yuiqnaiq sei Liljai sheel Gvceiq qu, Yulleq Naqxi ceef zeelzheel xail, Liqlail Yiq ceef zeelzheel xail, Yeseil xail, Diqqil Zail ceef zeelzheel ze xaigefli'la xail, Weiqsi Liqsu ceef zeelzheel xail, Defqi xail, Nvljai Liqsu ceef zeelzheel ze Gulsai Dvfleq cvf Nvl ceef zeelzheel xail, Seelcuai sei Liaiqsai Yiqceef zeelzheel ze Yaiqyuaiq xail, Mufli Zail ceef zeelzheel xail, Paizheehua sheel Yaiqbiai xail, Gaizee Zail ceef zeelzhee ze Bataiq xail nef Sizail zeelzheel qu Maiqkai xail cheehu ddiuq zzeeq. Wuduwuq seil "Naq" "Naqxi" "Naqssee" "Naqhail" bbei sel, ebbei sherlbbei tei'ee loq seil "Maqsa yiq" "Moso maiq" "Molso" "Moqso" "Moso" "Moq" "Moqdiq" "Mo" cheehu bbei teiq jeldiu. 1956 niaiq, miqceef ceefmiq tee teyif bbei "Naqxi" sel. Xofze nee yaijel bbel ceeq mei, Naqxi cvf nef ebbei sherlbbei ngelggeeq guefja gge sibef hoqhuaiq chee loq gge gv Ciaisseiq chee zzi bber coq bber gv zhul ddee reeggv gge qu waq zeel, <Hel hail sv·Si ciai zuail> <Huaq yaiq gueq zheel> <Sv zu guai jil> cheehu tei'ee loq nee sel mei, Naqxi cvf gge epvzzee chee hoqhuaiq ddiuqkol nee "Yichee meeq juq bber bbel Miqjai ggeq zul tv, seil sinaiq juq lei bber bbel Yaqgujai yibbiq ddiuq tv, bbil ejuq nimei ggvq juq lei bber bbel haiqyibbiq ggeqzul gge nimeitv nef nimeiggvq juq tv" zeel, Taiq caq chee rheeq seil eyi gge Diai Cuai Zail gai teiq zulzu gge ddiuqkol teiq zzeeq seiq. Taiqdail gaizherl gai, Naqxi ceef nee zzeeq gge ddiuq chee eyi gge Yaiqyuaiq chee loq nee liulggv hof. Taiqcaq gaizherl nee sheel bbel Yuaiqcaq gaizherl tv, Naqxi ceef zzeeq ddiuq gge liulggv chee Yaiqyuaiq nee mail ddeeq bbel eyi gge Yiggvddiuq tv seiq. Yuaiq Miq ddeegaiq, Yiggvddiuq nee liulggv hof gge Naqxi ceef zzeeqddiuq gge jizil selhuil jjaiq gai tv seiq. Cicaq gaizherl gge gaitv gui'lieq nee qucaq chee lahal gai daho gai meelmee mai, Naqxi ceef bieif gge miqcvf gol daho, Habaq nef bieif gge sasvl miqcvf la Naqxi ceef gol gai daho gge jjuq. 2010 N dil luq ceel quaiqguef sseiqke pvcaf tejil gol nee liuq mei, Naqxi ceef xikee tee 326295 gvl jjuq ye.

Ddee. Seiseel gol nee me berl gge Naqxi diaizif

Naqxi ceef gge gvzif tei’ee loq chee Naqxi ceef gge ddumuq ozzei ddeebeil teiq jeldiu, Naqxi tei'ee nee berl gge nef Habaq tei'ee nee berl gge Naqxi ceef gge liqshee veiqhual teiq faiyil gge tei'ee, dobbaq jeq, pvzee, duilliaiq, serjel lvjel cheehu nef gvbee, zzerbee, jaibee cheehu koku nee mailji mail zul bbel ceeq gge ddeehe bbei kuq yi seiq. Tei'ee cheehu loq Naqxi tei'ee zziuq nee berl, ddeecherl gguq ddeecherl mail zul bbel ceeq gge gvzif cheehu nee lahal ddeemaiq ee. Naqxi ceef gge tei’ee seil Dobbaq tei’ee (Rerko tei’ee nef Ma’lil masa tei’ee kuq yi) nef Ggeqbbaq tei’ee nisiuq jju. Dobbaq tei’ee nee berl gge Dobbaq jeq eyi ddiuq loq 1000 siuq hal, 3 mee cai ggeq lol jju, ggeqbbaq tei’ee nee berl gge jeq la ddeehu jju. Dobbaq tei'ee nef Ggeqbbaq tei'ee bbei "zujal jidiai nee zeiq gge tei'ee" waq, Dobbaq jal gge Dobbaq nee kee zul, jeq berl loq zeiq bbeeq, dobbaq ddeehu nef dobbaq tei'ee see gge quiqzul ddeehu nee tei'ee zziuq cheesiuq zeiq bbei cher'ee liuq tei'ee, pvzee tei'ee, qilyof tei'ee, konil tei'ee, jelzeiq jeldiu cheehu berlber, mail teiq ziul gge dobbaq tei'ee loq, dobbaq jeq nee bbeeq ssua, zeizeiq tei'ee berl gge jjaiq me jju. Dobbaq tei’ee chee goqwa gol nee liuq seil wasiuq bbei bbiu tal: (1) Neeq meil oq meil kvlssee zhul tei’ee. Mee biuq, yuq biuq, seel kvq, gga biuq, nol biuq, oqmei biuq cheehu bbei yi. (2) Ceeq ddiul kuaq pil tei’ee. Zvyal seil dol keel ddoq bvl, bbv biuq, chel gvq, gguq bvl zza bvl cheehu waq. (3) Xikai xingvl tei’ee. Xikai nef xingvl, Sherller ngvl, Lamu ngvl, derq ngvl, cee ngvl yeq ngvl cheehu yi. (4) Zeezeeq gulgu tei’ee. Zeezeeq gulgu gge Dobbaq tei’ee sseiddeq ddeebeil jju, zeeq nef paiq gge bee la bbeeq, lv paiq, geeq zeeq, yilmu seeq, bbaiqmai dol, bageq zeeq cheehu bbei tal, xikai, chermei sseeq, jjiqceel ddaiqssaiq, ssuif jiheq, gguqcer jju, xi shee, meekuel gvgai cheehu sher jju seil <Nilwa liuq tei’ee> <Bageq zeeq tei’ee> <Yilmu seeq liuq tei’ee> cheehu tei’ee liuq paiq tal. (5) Holho nolno gge tei’ee. Coco ggegge, cher’ee, zzerbee cheehu gge tei’ee la jju, <Dobbaq comuq> <Cher’ee siuq liuq tei’ee> <Gguqqil gu> cheehu waq. Dvq neeq mee gge Dobbaq tei’ee cheehu tee, Naqxi epvzzee nee see mei ee mei waq, zujal, liqshee, yuyaiq veiqzeel, veiqxof yilsvf, zeilzheel zefxof, tiaiveiq liffaf, jizil, yiyof, selhuil seihof cheehu goqwa bbei kuqjuq yi, “Naqxi ceef gvdail shelhuil gge befko cuaiqsu” bbei sel. Yaiq Fufquaiq jalsel nee teiqggv nee berl gge tei'ee <Deba jal te'luil> loq nee ssei ee bbei sel mei: "Tosheeq meelsheeq nvq, meelkeeq nee sul naq sei gge tei'ee cheehu loq, Naqxi epvzzee nee meekuel gol nef xiyuq gol gge seeddv, mee neiq ddiuq, xi neiq ceeqderq gol gge sher, ddiuq loq ggvzzeiq nef sher chee waq gge tvgv beelgv cheehu sher gol lei ggaihee zaq, lei seeddv zzeiqyi bbei teiq sel, xi nef svq golggee gge sher ssei ee bbei seeddv, mee nef ddiuq, xi lei jiheq lei mul lei gguq lei shee cheehu sher ddvddv jerljer, halsherq gge nilwa loq Naqxi xiyuq gge jjeq neiq zaq cheebeil teiq jeldiu.

Naqxi ceef gge dobbaq tei'ee loq seiseel gol nee berl me waq gge tei'ee ddeehu jju mel see, tei'ee cheehu sul'oq me nilniq, goqwa me nilniq, eyi see gge seil seesiuq bbei bbiuq tal: Ddeesiuq seil ddv gge, lvba gol nee ddv gge nef meel zeel ser zeel gol nee teiq ddv gge, Dobbaq tei'ee nee ddv gge ddeemaiq nee. 1934 N, Fai Guefyuq siaisei nee Yibbiq ku zzoqlvq ddeezzoq bbvq nee, 400 kvl gai Miqdail ggeqbbaq tei'ee teiq ddv gge lvba ddoq jji, “ssee sherq hal yi” shel cheehu geezheeq waq, mei lvba chee'lvl 1951 N sseeggv ddv cheekaq pielnil bbel hee seiq. Eyi elggeeq nee see chee, Liljai sheel Yulleq Naqxi ceef zheelzheel xail Basai xai, Tafceiq xai, Seelcuai sei Liaiqsai Yiq ceef zeelzheel ze Mufli Zailceef zeelzheel xail Oqyal xai loq Dobbaq tei'ee teiq ddv gge wazheeqbie nef feiqlv ddeehu jju. Oqyal Naqxi ceef rerko xi nee daqrhu ceel nieq ddvqbbv ddaddaq Dobbaq tei'ee teiq ddv gge lv ddeebie zeeq ddu, xi ddeehu seil yagoq kukee, ceesaiq derl bbiuq kee la zeeq, ceeq ddiul zza bvl gge geezheeq teiq ddv. Liljai sheel bof'vq yuail loq Dobbaq tei'ee ddv gge wazheeqbie nef Dobbaq tei'ee, ggeqbbaq tei'ee duilzal gge yilsuaf diabai ddeehu jju. Nisiuq cheesiuq seil Naqxi Dobbaq mufpaiq hual waq. Mufpaiq hual Naqxi geezheeq seil "kolbbaiq" sel, Dobbaq nee biubiuq sulsu sher bbei seil, Dobbaq tei'ee nef tvqsiail nee serkol gol teiq hual chee gol sel neeq, ebbei sherlbbei gge yuaiqshee huilhual yilsvf ddeesiuq waq, Dobbaq yilsvf gai gvyuq neeq cheezherl loq gge ggvzzeiq waq. <Yuiqnaiq sasvl miqceef fei zheezheef diaizif julzei·zufmuf jaidvq luil yif> sel gge tei'ee cheecai loq, Liljai sheel bo'vf guai nee teiq ggvqsee gge ssei zeiguil gge Naqxi dobbaq kolbbaiq ddeehu kuq tei se. Seesiuq seil juaizuq hual, Naqxi geezheeq “pv'laq zai” bbei sel, Dobbaq nee lvba gol nee tv gge ssalcher zeiq yeel peiq gol teiq hual gge pv'laq gol sel, sseiddeq ddeebeil jju, zai sherq, ddeepeil zai nef sseipeil zai cheehu jjaiq nisiuq jju, chee tee Dobbaq huilhual yilsuf lahal lahal ee gge ddeezherl loq tvmei waq. Zai ddeepeil gol heiqddeeq ddeezzer mewaf gga'laq ddeezzer hual, heiqddeeq tee Saqyi weddei, Yiggvq aggeq, Heiqddee wo'perq nef Dibba sherllo, Dogeq, Yemaq cheehu waq.Zai ezee ddeepeil megua heiq ddeezzer nef heiq xul ddiuq teiq hual. Guefja tvqsvguai, Naiqji tvqsvguai, Zuyai miqceef dalxof, Yuiqnaiq sei sasvl miqceef gvzif zei'li guihual bailgusheef, Liljai Deba veiqhual yaijelyuail, Liljail sheel bof'vqyuail, Liljai Yulleq Naqxiceef zeelzheel xail tvqsvguai cheehu loq bbei bbeebbeeq neenee nee Naqxi Dobbaq pv'laq zai ddeehu teiq ggvqsee. Eyi cheeguq loq ceefbai gge <Yuiqnaiq sasvl miqceef gvzif zeibei jifceiq> <Yuiqnaiq sasvl miqceef huilhual diaizif jifceiq> <Yuiqnaiq sasvl miqceef cuaiqte huilhual> cheehu tei'ee loq bbeiqpv ssua gge pv'laq zai ddeehu caiseif bbei pef bbil teiq keel.

Ni. Naqxi dobbaq heiqreepiq gge goqwa nef zeizeiq

Heiqddee seil dobbaq zai loq zuil yuaiqshee, zuil dailbia sil jju gge sherddeeq gge ggvzzeiq waq, Naqxi dobbaq nee xikai xingvl cheekaq zeiq gge ssei shersher gge hual ddeeddee waq. Heiqreepiq gge yilsee tee xi me jjuq pil seil dobbaq nee xi shee cheegvl zzee bbei sher lei perq, heiq ddiuq bbee dder gge sseeggv lei sheeq yel, tee gge oqhei chee niwe ceiqhol ddiuq nee muqdiul lei berf ceeq, ddiuqloq nee xi bbei lei jiheq, me waf meqzeel bvlbv bbel heiq ddiuq tv hee zherq.

Heiqreepiq chee niwe ceiqhol ddiuq, xi ddiuq, heiq ddiuq see ddiuq bbiu, zulzu bbei xi shee bbil jji dder gge ceeq ddiuq wecei gai chee ddiuq ---- jjuq naq ggvjjuq teiq hual, dobbaq jal nee vq mei, xi chee ddiuq loq jjuq cheekaq me hof gge bbeidoq jju, ceesaiq kol jji, shee bbil chee ddiuq gai lei jji mai seil, sul kuaq xi rer gge "leiq cel" ceeq nee gai teiq hu lee gvl zeel. Tee gguq seil "niwe" ddiuq, "yi ddal" ddiuq loq tv, dobbaq jal loq xi shee bbil lei zuaisheel gvl sel gge guainiail jju seiq, teiq jjuq cheekaq ceesaiq siul jji, xi gol lei seesee agaiqssee siul, xi kv bo kail, geezheeq kuaq sel xi hail, ddee coq'o mil cherpiel, ggv'laq bbei mei jiqkee me mul, mi keel jjuq bberq, jjihoq nielnie cheehu bbei me ddu gge bbei, sel me tal gge sel, shee bbil "niwe" ddiuq, "yi ddal" ddiuq loq nee lei jiheq zo waq. Dobbaq nee xi shee oqhei gol lei baba, ceeq ddiuq gai gol zzaiq, niwe ddiuq gge sui kee nee oqhei lei sherl ceeq, seiq zaq mei gge "bbei ceeq ssee ddiuq" xi ddiuq lei tv, oqhei cheehu sseiggv jjeq bbel ceeq bbil xi lei bie. Mailgguq seil, heiq ddiuq tv gge ku mail pu, heiq jjuq sherjjuq, heiq heel sherheel jju gge heiqddiuq tv, oqhei lei bvl bbel seecerq seeddiuq heiqddiuq tv. Dobbaq nee baqnv 16-30 liqmi yi, sherqnv 15 mi yi gge peiq ddeekeeq gol nee, ssissi daidai gge lvba ssalcher zeiq, ssei guezhee gge laqmee nee, xingvl gge sseeggv ddeehe bbei muqdiul teiq seel. Heiqddee gol xi, heiq, ceeq 360 gvl hal nef ddvzzeeq kozzeeq gge 70 siuq hal teiq hual. Ngelggeeq guefja meisuf shee gol zuil sherq gge zai bbei sel, “ebbei sherlbbei zujal huilhual dilyif caiq juail” sel miqzzeeq.

Xi chee xiyuq yalji gge ddeeni zherl loq, biruq jiheq nieq, ggeqdiuq nieq, sher bail nieq, abbamei bbei nieq, kasheel ka mai, lobbei ggeq tv, lei shee gol tv gge ddeecherl loq, ddee pa'la gge biubiuq sulsu ddumuq jju, chee tee xi ddeegvl chee hual gol gai teiq paipai, sher jju bbei zzaiq cheetv sel neeq mei waq. Naqxi ceef nee xi ddeegvl gge mie golyi nef ddeehual golyi gge sher jju nieq, xikai xingvl sel ddumuq cheetv gol nee, dobbaq nee "heiqreepiq" gguq zul, shee bbil cheegvl gge oqhei seel bbel sheel gge ddeeddiuq tv, chee seiqmei yagoq xihual, ddeebbei xihual golggee seiq bbei dder lei bbei, xi shee gol rerrer qi'qi jju me zherq, xi shee bbil gguq seiq waq ddu mei seiq lei waq zherq. Yiqsheel bbei cheekaq, dobbaq nee heiqreepiq gai teiq ku yi, dobbaq ddeehe bbei seiq xul ddu mei ddaddaq teiq xul yi, ddeegvl gguq ddeegvl bbei <Heiqreepiq> cu, xi shee cheegvl zzee bbei sher piq, heiq ddiuq bbee gge sseeggv sel yel, oqhei niwe ddiuq gge ceeq nee moq me zherq, ddeediul gguq ddeediul bbei ggeq jji hee zherq, bbeiceeqssee ddiuq tv seil xi bbei lei jiheq zherq, me waf bvl bbel heiq ddiuq tv zherq. Cheehu bbei nieq, dobbaq nee <Comuq> gguq zul bbei coco ggegge dder mel see. Heiqreepiq zeiq gge ddumuq seil Naqxi ceef gge saizail zheeldvl ddee gaibiail nee ddeehu me nilniq seiq. Gainieq muq jjil bbei chee rheeq, heiqreepiq tee muqjjil ddaiq loq nee, xi shee gge gu'liu kee nee eezzeeqdee juq mail kail bbei ku. "Gai tv gui lieq" bbil gguq, Naqxi muq me jjil bbei zhee bbi lei nv, seil heiqreepiq la haiqdal gu'liu kee nee lazzeeqdee juq mail lei ku.

Seeq. Naqxi dobbaq heiqreepiq gge veiqhual nuilhaiq nef jalzheef

Naqxi ceef chee Taiqcaq gai waq chee rheeq nee Zuguef yuqzzeeqdee ddiuqkol gge diai cuai zail zulzu gvq zeeq, Habaq, Naqxi, Ggvzzeeq, Leibbv, Leeseel, Yiq ceef, Bbe, Nvlceef cheehu miqceef bbei ddeeddiuq nee xiyuq, me nilniq gge rheeq loq zzi'qu coqhual bberbber, ggv'laq bbei jjijji, zzeeqbbuq susuq, ejuq me nilniq gge zujal cuaiqbol nef koqsail cheehu nee miqceef gozolggee zzeezzee bbeeq, veiqhual ja'lieq la bbeeq ssua. Cisiq me nilniq gge veiqhual ddeeweil jju gge ddiuq nee tv gge Naqxi dobbaq heiqreepiq, ssei cerf ssei siuq gge zujal veiqhual gai daho bbel ceeq, beijal, fvqjal gge veiqhual goqwa lahal ddeemaiq bbeeq, gof miqceef jjijji bbil nee nee nge gguq soq nge nee nee gguq soq, nilniq gv bbeeq chee tee waq seiq.

Naqxi dobbaq heiqreepiq chee sseiggv goqwa yi, kuqjuqgoq dilyuf guai, luiqli guai, seimil guai cheehu veiqhual guainiail nef veiqhual biadaf bee yi, chee tee Naqxi ceef wuduwuq nee see cheehu keedvq gol nee, rujal, sheefjal, yildvl jal, beijal cheehu me nilniq gge veiqhual gai daho bbel ceeq bbei bie gge waq, veiqhual me nilniq nef holho chee zelddee ssua, muftai nee ddeenitv ddee sel neeq: Ddeetv, heiqreepiq nee teiq faiyil gge seimil guai, liqhuiq guai chee fvqjal gge "saigail luqdal" luil, shee bbil lei seeq, ga bbei ga ddoq cheehu guainiail nee yixai gol nee tv gge ggvzzeiq waq. Dobbaq jal nee vq mei, teiq jjuq gge cheemie sei pil, "niwe cualddiuq" nee lei jiheq gvl, xi kai xi ngvl nieq, < Heiqreepiq > jeq biuq sei bbil, <Niwe cualddiuq> biuq dder melsee. Chee tee teiq zelddee bbei fvqjal gge "wuciul luqdal" sel cheebee nee yixai mai, fvqjal nee sel seil xi teiq jjuq cheekaq gge bbeidoq gol nee, niwe, hasser ceeq, ceesaiq, xi, mee nef axe'loq cualsiuq loq lei jiheq gvl. Heiqreepiq loq nee teiq sel gge heiqjjuq sherjjuq, heiqheel sherheel gge heiqddiuq la, fvqjal beezee loq neeq yi gge Xumiqsai ddaddaq xuqheel sherheel haiqjjuq sherjjuq sel chee gol biebie. Xi shee bvlbv bbel sseizaq mei ddiuq ---- seecerqseeq heiqddiuq tv sel cheebee seil, <Da zheel dvl luil> ggvcai cheecai loq nee sel gge "Xumiqsai suaqnv holmee ludvq yeqxuiq yi, ggeqdol seecerqseeq meezzaiq jju" sel cheebee gol nilniq. Yaiq Fvfquaiq jalsel nee sel seil "Naqxi ceef seecerqseeq heiqddiuq sel cheetv chee yildvl jal nee yixai mai, zail cuaiq fvqjal nee cuaiq bbel dobbaq jal loq tv keel mei zaq" zeel. Nitv, heiqreepiq chee Ggvzzeeq gge veiqhual nee yixai ddeeq, beijal veiqhual nef zail cuaiq fvqjal gge yixai nee ddeeq ssua seiq. Heiqreepiq loq nee jai mei, xi shee bbil ceeq ddiuq nee jjeqshee jjeqfvq, mailgguq seil maperq bbaq ceiqsee bbaq, heimei ceiqseel pei, dduqlv ceiqsee dduq, doma ceiqseel ge, xulzzerq ceiqsee zzerq, bbalbba ceiqsee bbaq, vlssi ceiqseel mei teiq hual gge zzijjeq la'ler ddiuq tv, ddiuqloq ezee sher me gua "ceiseeq" waq chee beijal gol nee ceeq. Chee dal me ssaf gge, heiqreepiq loq nee sel gge xishee bbil waddiuq nee lei jihe, nimeitv juq, xi chee gv perq loq nee tv; yicheemeeq juq, xi chee mil nee bul mil nee xiq; nimeiggvq juq, heiq chee bbaqkoq loq nee jjuq; hoggv'loq juq, heiq chee zzeerq gv nee jjuq, beezee cheehu <Sizail dvl waiq ji> loq nee sel gge luaisei, taisei, hualsei, sheefsei chee lultv lei jiheq bee gol nilniq. Seeqtv, heiqreepiq Habaq veiqhual teifseif gge luiqli guai sosoq, wuduwuq gge veiqhual gol gai zzeezzeeq. Heiqreepiq loq nee sel gge ceeqddiuq nef zziul jju xi gol biqtvl sel chee, <Yullif baca quailsheel veiq> <Yullif ca cuaisheel jeq> cheehu tei'ee loq nee yi gol nilniq, Ggvzzeeq gge <Geqsal'er waiq zuail> loq nee teiq sel gge 24 ddiuq xi biqtvl ddiuq tee, fvqjal gge "cei kuaq" gol nilniq gv jju, chee gol nee liuq tv mei, zuhuaq miqcvf chee gamei bbei gol ggeq ddeeq gge zzi'qu waq, gamei mu, gamei ddiul, gamei bbei, eneiq megua nvlmei ga ddee'liu yi, geezheeq gamei sel, gamei sher bbei, chee seifsee ga lei ddee tal meq.

Naqxi dobbaq heiqreepiq chee sseisiuq gge veiqhual gai daho bbel ceeq gge ozzei waq, Naqxi cuaiqte veiqhual yilsvf loq gge ggv ssua ggvzzeiq waq, tee gge veiqhual nef yilsvf jalzheef seil sel me dder seiq. Tei'ee cheecai tee Liljai sheel bof'vqyuail loq teiq ggvqsee gge heiqreepiq seelddee nef Pumi ceef gge taflaiqtvq ddeedi teiq keel gge ddeecai waq, tei'ee cheecai tee, goq tal keeq gv see, gv see neiq ggvf waq. Chee gguq miqceef xof, miqceef shee, miqceef yilsvf cheehu juq lahal ggv gge tei'ee muqdiul tv yelhol!

神路图（一）

神路图（一）
尺寸：长 1435 厘米，宽 34 厘米
收藏单位：丽江市博物院

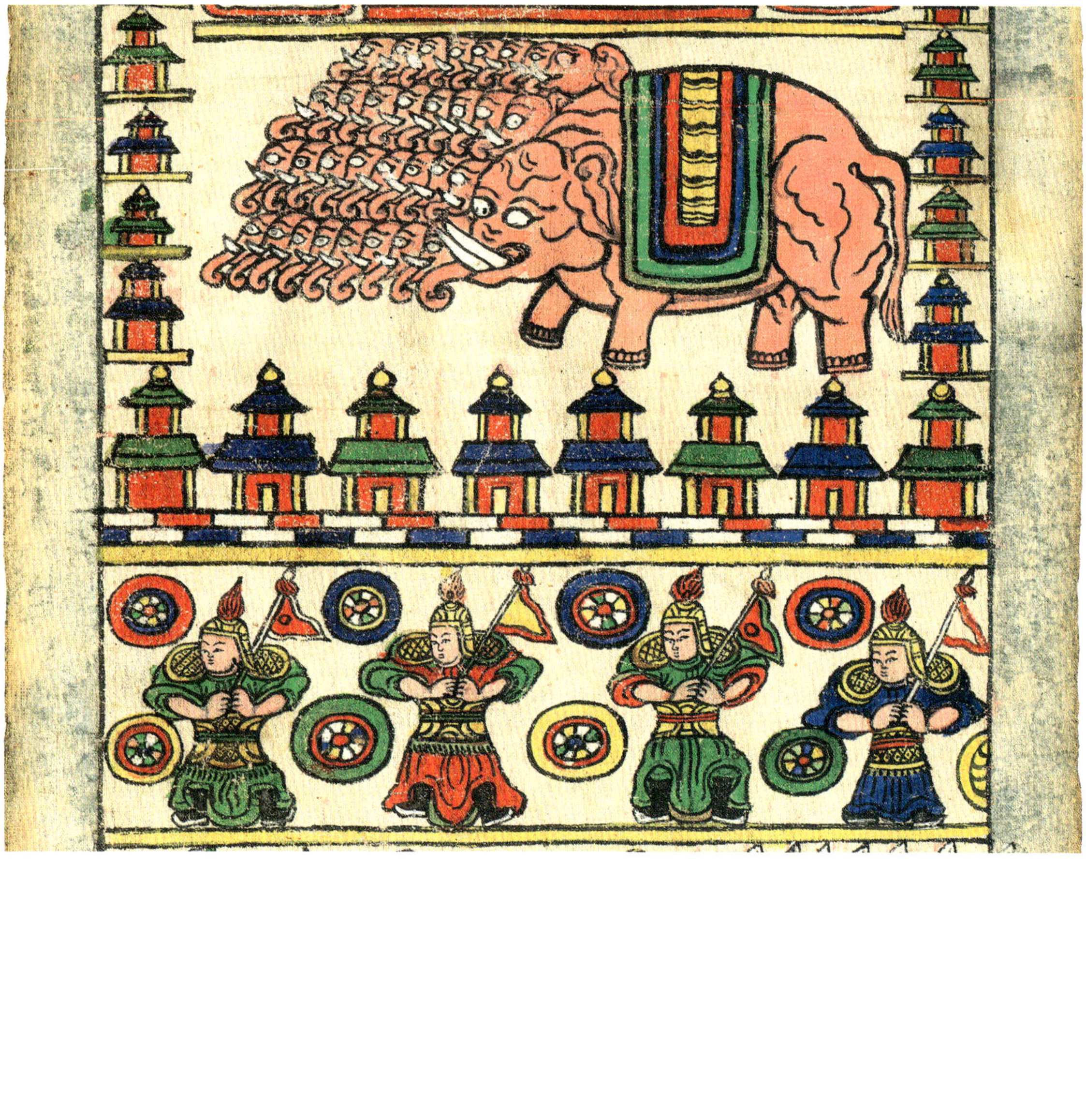

神路图（二）

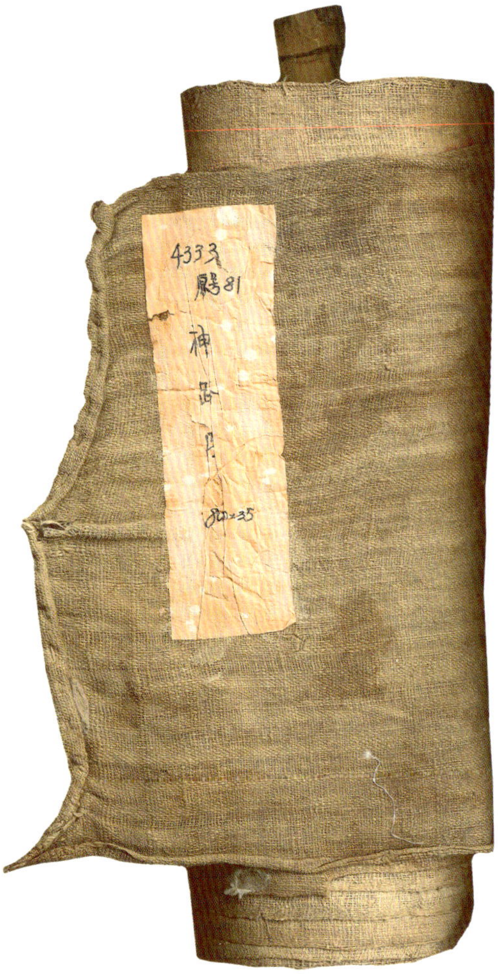

神路图（二）
尺寸：长 800 厘米，宽 35 厘米
收藏单位：丽江市博物院

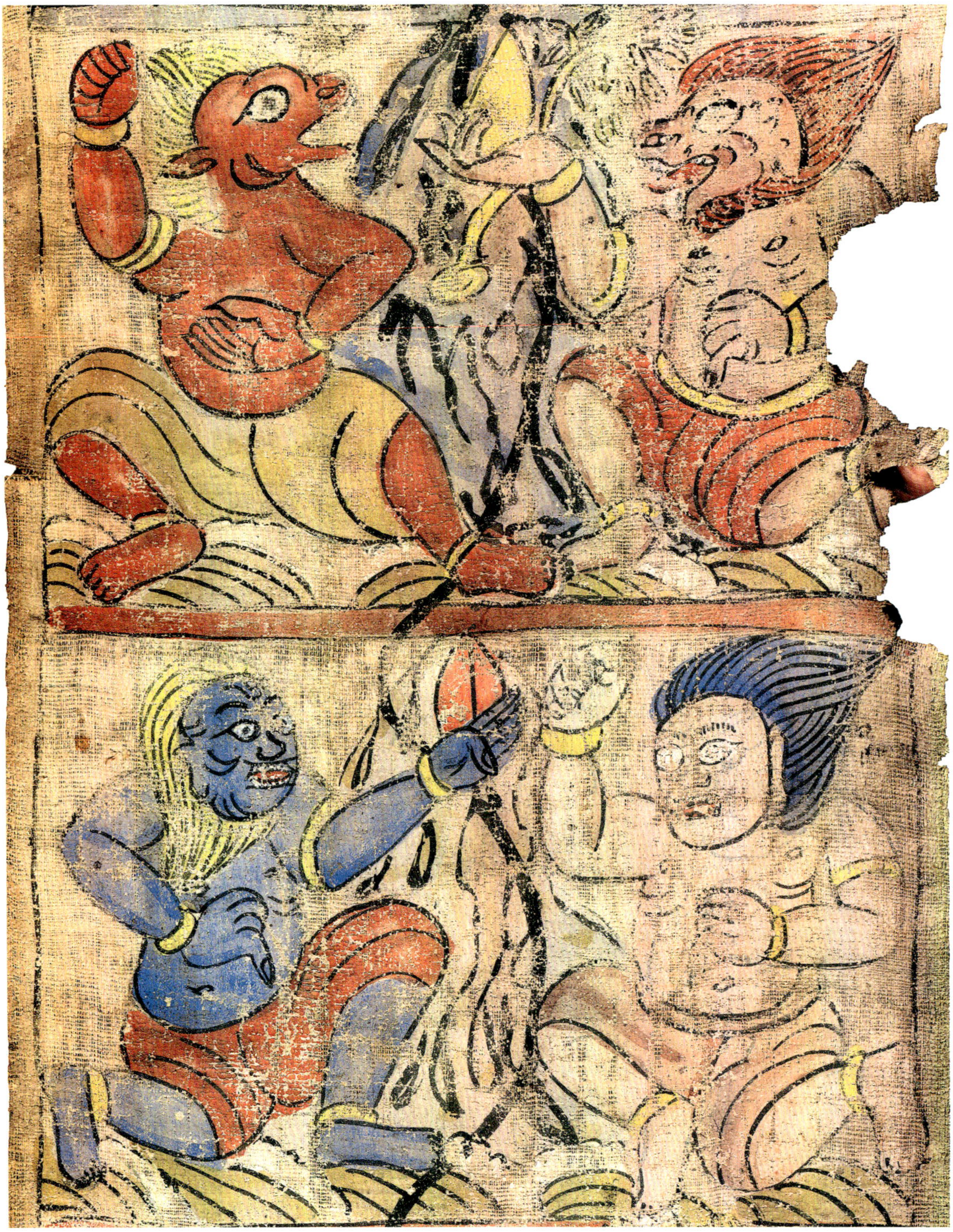

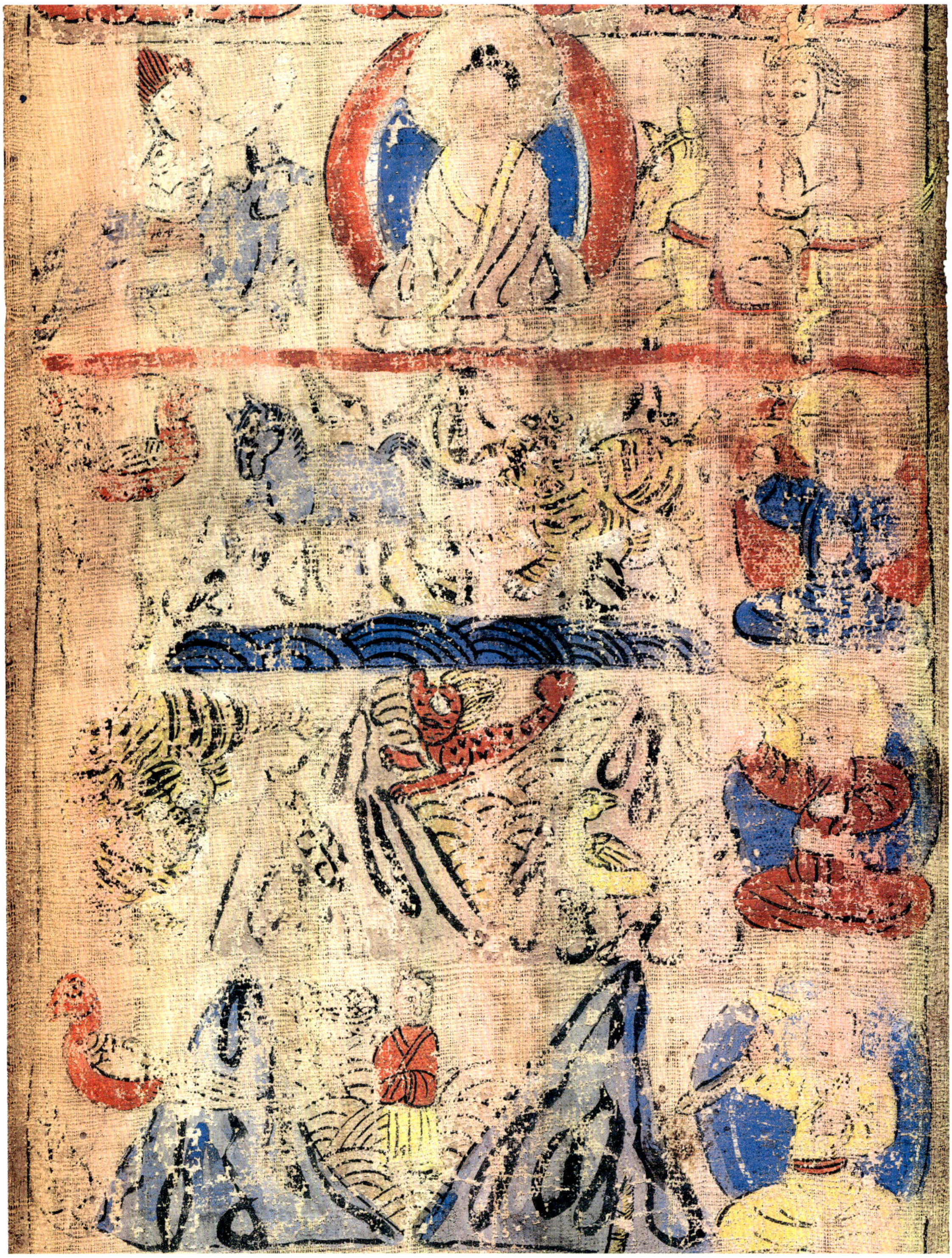

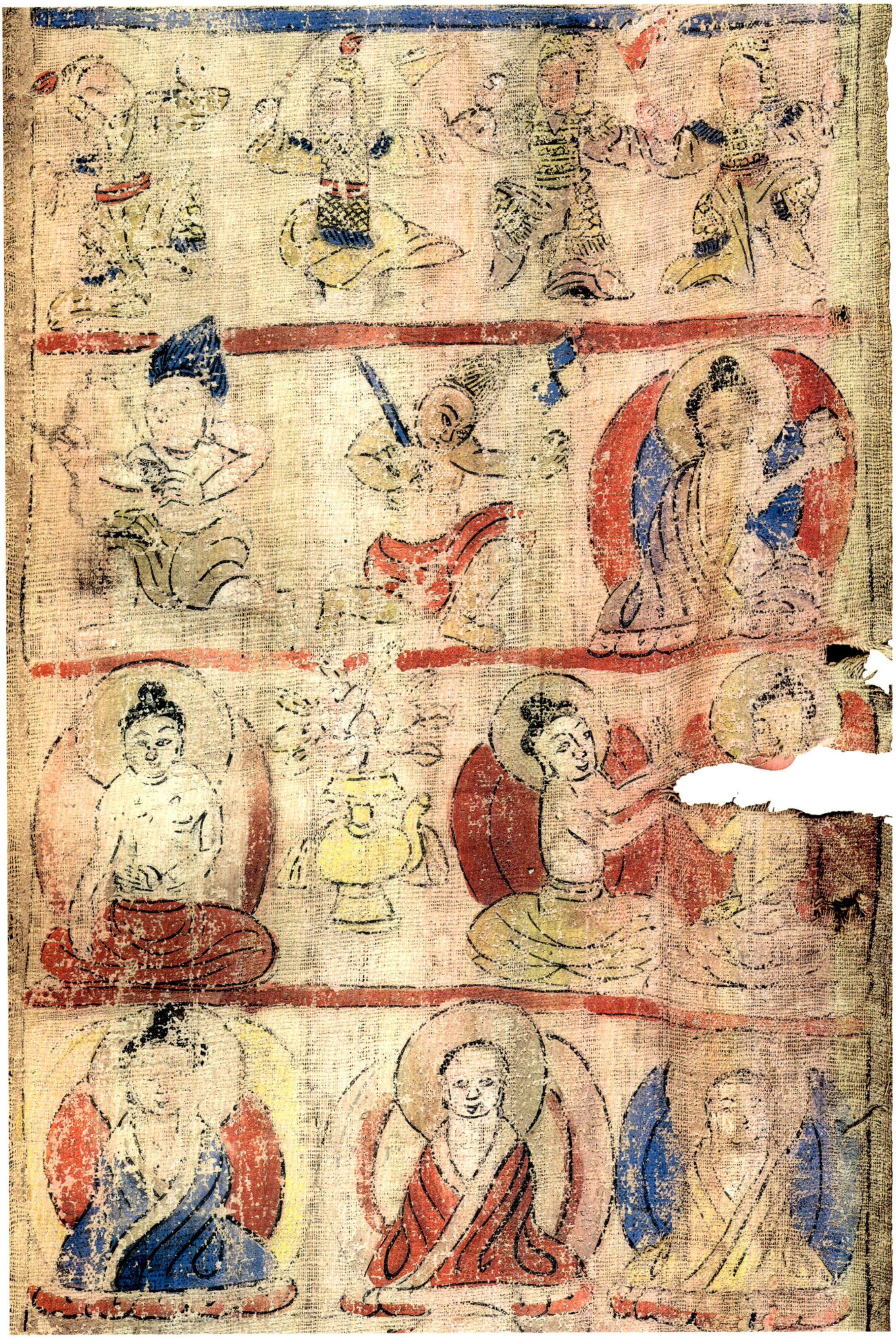

神路图（三）

神路图（三）
尺寸：长 1100 厘米，宽 26.5 厘米
收藏单位：丽江市博物院

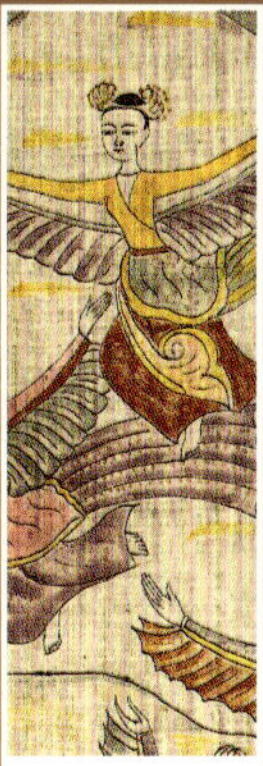

云南少数民族非纸质典籍聚珍

YUNNAN SHAOSHU MINZU FEIZHIZHI DIANJI JUZHEN

傣族布幡

傣族布幡概述

傣族是一个历史悠久的民族，有本民族的语言和古老文字，傣文分为傣泐文、傣那文、傣绷文和傣端文四种文字。傣文在傣族地区流传广泛，故而有大量历史文献、神话传说、史诗歌谣、民间文献等古籍传世，傣族布幡是最具艺术性、多样性的傣族古籍门类之一。

一、琳琅纷呈的傣族非纸质典籍

傣族古籍是指傣族在历史上形成的文献典籍、碑刻铭文及口头传承资料等，内涵丰富、形制多样。其中，用铁笔在贝多罗树叶上刻写的贝叶经，用绵纸、构皮纸抄写的纸质古籍和口传古籍数量最多、流传最广。传世傣族古籍数量众多，云南省内各大图书馆、博物馆、古籍办、研究所，傣族分布区各大南传上座部寺院等都有一定数量的收藏，尚有大量傣族古籍散布民间，但摸清傣族古籍家底仍是一项需经年之功方能完成的工作。傣族古籍包罗万象，涉及社会生活的方方面面。按当前掌握的资料，傣族古籍的内容大体包括佛教经典、哲学、法律法规、神话传说、史诗、叙事长诗、民间故事、歌谣、语言文字、农业、历法、医药、建筑、舞蹈、绘画等十七类。[1]

傣族古籍以其浩瀚的储量、广博的内容、延续的传承闻名于世，其中历史悠久、形制多样、珍品众多和最具代表性的非纸质典籍是银刻、贝叶经、布幡和象牙经等。贝叶经，傣语称作“坦兰”，是用铁笔刻写在经过特制的贝多罗树叶上的经文，我国傣族地区发现的贝叶经有巴利文本和傣文本，傣族人民将贝叶经称作“运载傣族历史走向光明的一叶神舟”。《云南少数民族非纸质典籍聚珍·竹木简牍类二》收录了入选第一批《国家珍贵古籍名录》的傣族民间叙事长诗《章相》和傣族佛经故事《桑玛

① 国家民族事务委员会全国少数民族古籍整理研究室编：《中国少数民族古籍总目提要·傣族卷·讲唱类》，民族出版社 2019 年版，第 2—12 页。

雅帕拉》两部贝叶经珍本。使用银片记事是傣族的传统记事方法，人们会在银片上用傣文或巴利文记录重大事件，傣文银刻留存较少，但具有重要的文物价值和研究价值。《云南少数民族非纸质典籍聚珍·金石器物类》便收录了云南省博物馆和西双版纳傣族自治州勐海县文化馆收藏的数件傣族银刻珍品。此外，象牙经、傣族布幡等都是珍贵的傣族非纸质典籍。

二、傣族布幡的形制和种类

傣族布幡是傣族社会生活中使用的各类布制旌旗的总称，依形制可分为云幡、幢、旗等，其中圆桶状者为幢，长片状者为幡，是傣族民俗活动中用于供奉和祭祀的供具与法器。佛经中认为:“佛陀则以智慧之幢，降伏一切烦恼之魔军。以幢象征摧破之义，故被视为庄严具。用于赞叹佛菩萨及庄严道场，……用于祈福或其它佛教仪式中。”[①]南传上座部佛教自东南亚传入我国后，主要在滇西、滇南区域，即德宏傣族景颇族自治州、西双版纳傣族自治州、红河彝族哈尼族自治州、普洱市、临沧市、保山市等地区流传。傣族布幡是南传上座部佛教本土化的产物，不仅是“民众礼佛活动中的赕品，是功德善举的载体”，亦是“以视觉形象阐释神话叙事的载体”，承担了“教化普罗大众、美化环境、传播大众审美以及传承多元文化的功能”[②]，更是傣族传统工艺与民间艺术的结晶、傣族传统文化的传承载体。

傣语中布幡音译为“统”“懂”“焕”“换”“听”“杂扎”等，称呼众多与其制作工艺及使用功能、场合不同有关。傣族布幡大部分由信众直接制作或委托创作并奉献给佛寺，少部分为南传上座部佛教僧侣亲自制作或委托民间手工艺人制作，多用于各类赕佛活动和寺庙装饰。赕佛也称为“做摆”，傣族认为“做摆”可以让人在死后到达佛国天堂。“做摆”时通常购买佛像、布幡、佛伞、佛经等用品，和其他钱物一起奉献给佛寺和僧人，“做摆”在傣族社会生活中发挥着重要作用。布幡作为主要的民俗用品也不断被创作、创新。

傣族布幡在材料、造型、风格色彩上表现各异，主要有织锦、刺绣、布画等，通

① 杨建军、崔岩：《唐代佛幡图案与工艺研究》，载《敦煌研究》2014 年第 2 期，第 1 页。

② 屈永仙：《傣族神话叙事与佛教艺术——以佛寺经画与剪纸为例》，载《民族艺术研究》2020 年第 3 期，第 40 页。

常幅宽20—60厘米，长短不一，最长的可达10米。通常为纵式幡画，图案或情节从上至下绘制，也有少量为横式幡画。纵式布幡在图案或故事情节改变的过渡之处，背面横穿有细小的竹片，以防幡卷拢，增强其立体垂悬效果。傣族布幡也呈现出明显的地域特色，西双版纳与德宏地区以织锦布幡见长。西双版纳傣锦多以白色为底，用红色或黑色纬线织成花纹；德宏傣锦则色调浓重，常用黑、红、翠绿等浓艳色线，掺以金丝棉线。临沧地区则以工艺精细、色彩艳丽的刺绣布幡闻名。刺绣布幡一般将长方形的刺绣片装订在纵式缎面布幡下端的正反两面，长度为120—150厘米，宽度为20—40厘米，绣片下端饰以丝坠。刺绣布幡色彩配置强烈明快，多选用橘黄、朱红、淡金黄等暖色绸缎作底，局部用金属珠或金线点缀，再用金银线绣出轮廓。西双版纳的布画故事幡极具特色。布画故事幡一般由傣族称为“章跌姆”的画匠或画师创作，在涂浆裱平磨光的布料上勾画轮廓，再着以颜色。“章跌姆”是擅长作画的民间艺人或者僧侣，不仅创作布画故事幡，也是南传上座部佛教佛寺壁画的创作者。傣族布画故事幡构思简洁、质朴，充满浓郁的民俗气息。画幅形制有单幅横式、双联竖式、多联竖式等多种。一般来说，色彩缤纷的布幡是敬献给佛祖的，白色长幡则是献给祖先和死去的亲人的，前者多挂于佛寺大殿内或两侧偏厦，后者多挂于佛寺旁的风尾竹竿上。

三、傣族布画故事幡的制作及功能

布画故事幡是傣族布幡中最具故事性、朴拙感和教化意义的文化遗存，也是表现场景故事的首选。

布幡的内容因制作工艺不同而有所不同，织锦布幡图案大多为人物、动植物图案的循环往复；刺绣布幡对材质和制作工艺有着严格要求，图案可简可繁；布画故事幡则对创作者的绘画水平有一定要求，讲究独特的创作技法与空间布局，使得布画故事幡更生动、丰富地展示场景故事。一般来说，场景故事只出现在刺绣布幡与布画故事幡中。绘制布画故事幡采用手工纺织的土布、天然的矿物质和植物颜料，以佛教教义、经典著作、佛教故事、佛教典故为题材进行创作，无严格的程式画法，有较大的创作空间，因创作者的不同，有的色彩奇丽、画面富丽，有的淡雅质朴、清新自然。造型上习惯“用鲜活的生活与景物阐释宗教内涵，充满了世俗味和人间情”，布画中的动植物、人物和生活场景都可以在现实生活中找到原型。

元文化交流整合的载体。布画故事幡描绘的场景故事通常是佛本生经故事，也是在傣族地区广泛流传的民间故事。如本书收录的布画故事幡描绘了在傣族地区家喻户晓的民间故事《千瓣莲花》中的经典情节。布幡卷首以简洁的笔触，描绘了天界的七个公主穿着羽衣来到人间的金湖戏水，七公主因羽衣被人藏起无法返回天界，与男子在人间结为夫妻。该故事采用了东南亚地区普遍流传的羽衣女情节，男子历经艰辛，在神龙和隐居僧人的帮助下最终夫妻团圆。其次，布画故事幡具有鲜明的世俗性与民族性，是傣族社会生活的真实写照。如本书收录的布画故事幡的十二幅画面中仅有两幅出现扮演智者或救助者的僧人形象，更多的是描绘了傣族人民的世俗生活，甚至有一幅细致描绘了赞哈表演的情景，最中间赞哈盘膝而坐，一人吹笛，一人手执纸扇半遮住脸歌唱，周围的听众表情如醉如痴。最后，布画故事幡是傣族文化传承的重要舞台与途径。一方面，它继承了傣族民间绘画艺术“天真淳朴、自由”的风格，构图不受时间、空间、情节的限制，自由表达，有的一幅只描述一个情节，有的两三个故事情节集中在一个画面内表现。另一方面，它在傣族社会生活中发挥了积极、向上的宣教功能。佛寺是傣族民俗文化不可缺少的场所，是傣族文化集中呈现的场域。傣族男性基本都有出家为僧、接受佛寺教育的经历，傣族女性则从幼年开始就到佛寺中听经、赕佛，“佛寺教育”在传统的傣族社会生活中发挥重要作用。故事布画幡不仅展现了南传上座部佛教的思想和传说，更以自身的艺术形象承载并传播着傣族的民间传说与故事，用图像的方式继承口传叙事的传统，使之成为传承傣族传统历史文化的重要载体，“故事世代相传，增强了人们对民族和国家的身份认同感”[①]。

傣族布画故事幡因制作不易，加之其特殊的民间使用习俗——到了年底就将陈旧的布幡集中销毁，相比织锦布幡、刺绣布幡而言，传世布画故事幡数量稀少。本书收录的云南省博物馆收藏的布画故事幡，绘制故事完整生动、年代较久，是稀见的傣族布画故事幡珍品。

① 刘朦：《傣族“孔雀公主”故事在佛寺景观中的呈现》，载《红河学院学报》2014年第4期，第4页。

[illegible]

[illegible]

[illegible]

[illegible]

[illegible]

[illegible]

[illegible]

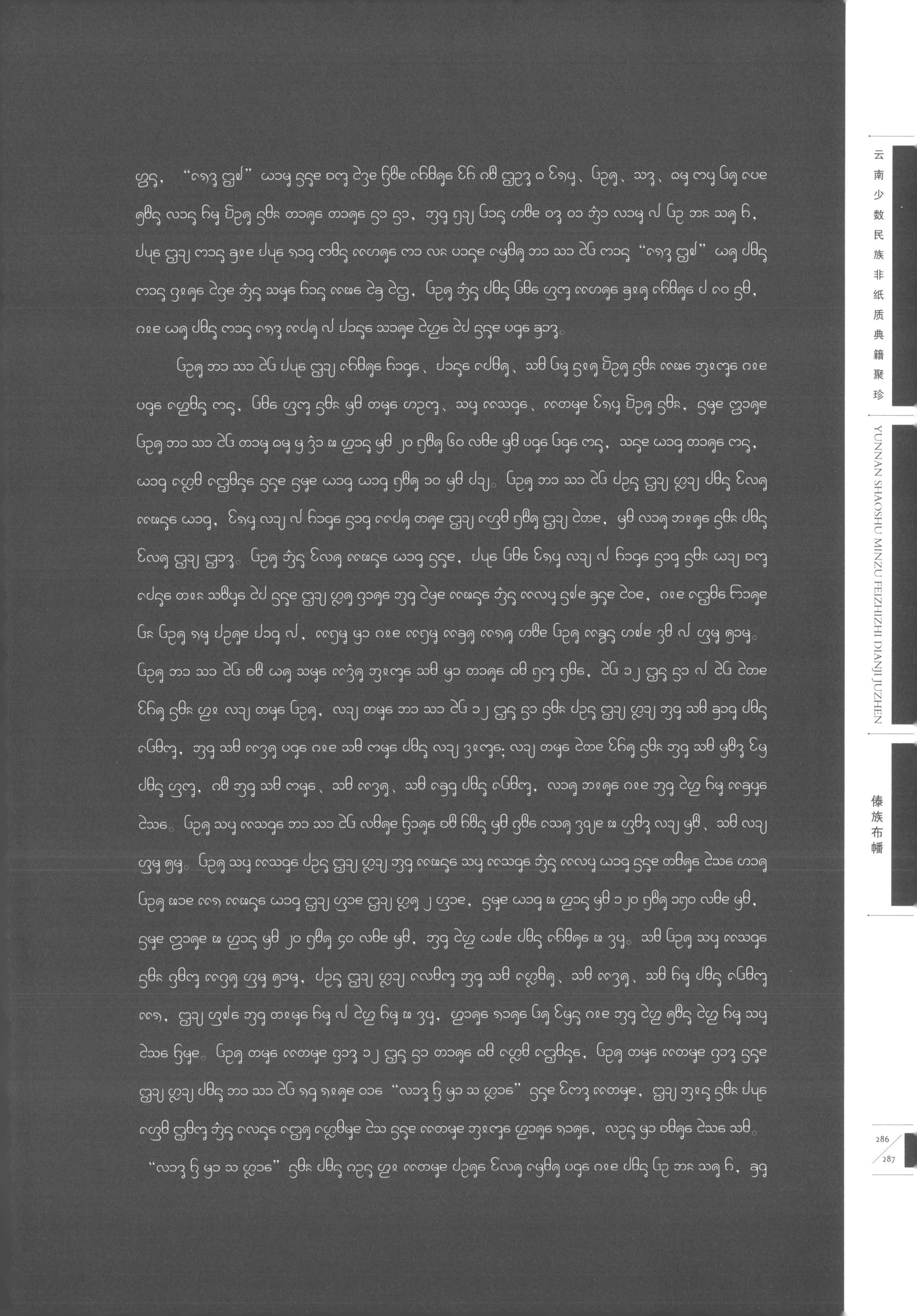

[illegible]

ᦵᦟᦙᦲᧂ ᦵᦡᦙᦲᧆ ᦖᦱᧃ ᦡᦱᦖᦲ ᦷᦎᦙᦲᧃ “ᦔᦸᧆ ᦆᦲᧈ ᦡᦴᧃ ᦓᦸᧆ ᦂᦙᦱᧃ ᦟᦲ ᦐᦳᧃᧃ ᦵᦟᦙᦲᧂ ᦖᦱ ᦶᦂᦲ ᦺᦋ ᦕᦲᦰ ᦷᦃᦸᧂ

ᦀᦲ ᦺᦑ ᦉᦱ ᦉ ᦑ, ᦎᦙᦲᧉ ᦺᦡ ᦕᦲᦰ ᦷᦒᦱᧉ ᦖ ᦑᦴᦰ ᦉᦱ” , ᦡᦳᧂ ᦼᦓᧉ ᦐᦲᧃ ᦶᦉᧁ、ᦎᦳᧃ ᦺᦖᦲ ᦵᦃᦲᧄ ᦆᦸᧆ、

ᦂᦳᧃ ᦏᦙᦲᧂ ᦂᦱᧃ ᦆᦲᧈ ᦡᦴᧃ ᦓᦸᧆ ᦂᦙᦱᧃ ᦂᦲᧈ ᦼᦂᧃ ᦡᦴᧃ ᦺᦑ ᦼᦑᧃ ᦔᦸ ᦵᦔᦸᧃ ᦓᦸ ᦐᦱ ᦺᦔᦲ ᦶᦔᦴᧃ ᦵᦡᦙᦲᧆ ᦔᦲᧈᦂᦸᧃ

ᦖᦱ。

ᦗᦳᧃ ᦔᦱᧁ ᦑᦳᧃ ᦡᦙᦱᧃ ᦵᦂᦙᦲᧂ ᦶᦃᧃ ᦶᦐᦸᧂ ᦷᦒᦱᧉ ᦵᦔᦙᦲ ᦵᦉ ᦟᦱᧁ, ᦋᦙᦲ ᦍᦸᧆ ᦆᦲᧈᦸᧆ ᦀᦱᧁ ᦞ ᦑ ᦞᦲᧉ ᦉᦙᦲᦴᧃ ᦗᦱᧂ

ᦆᦴᧃ ᦺᦑᦸ ᦐᦱ ᦂᦱᧃ。᧑、ᦗᦳᧆ ᦔᦱᧁ ᦡᦙᦱᧃ ᦆᦲᧈᦸᧆ ᦆᦲᧈᦳᧃ ᦓᦲᧈᦖᦲ ᦀᦱᧁ ᦞ ᦑ ᦷᦒᦱᧂ ᦵᦔᦙᦲ ᦷᦒᦱᧂ ᦔᦲᧈᦸᧆ ᦆᦴᧃ ᦺᦑᦸ ᦐᦱ ᦂᦱᧃ。

ᦎᦱᦖᦲ ᦼᦟᦸᧆ ᦵᦖᦙᦲᧆ ᦖᦱ ᦀᦱᧃ ᦷᦂᦸᧃ ᦑᦙᦲᧃ ᦍᦱᧂ ᦶᦎᦖᦲ ᦺᦉᧃ ᦗᦳᧆ ᦔᦱᧁ ᦑᦳᧃ ᦡᦙᦱᧃ ᦂᦱᧃ ᦔᦱ ᦼᦔᦸᧂ, ᦐᦱᦸᧂ ᦡᦙᦱᧃ

ᦷᦂᦸᧃ ᦑᦙᦲᧃ ᦍᦱᧂ ᦼᦟᦸᧆ ᦵᦖᦙᦲᧆ ᦔᦲᧃ ᦉᦙᦲᦴᧃ ᦶᦃᧃ ᦶᦐᦳᧃ ᦂᦱᦸᧂ ᦺᦡ ᦔᦱᧃ ᦵᦖᦙᦲᧆ ᦺᦗ ᦑᦳᧃ ᦟᦲ。ᦵᦗᦲ ᦖᦱ ᦗᦳᧆ

ᦔᦱᧁ ᦶᦐᦸᧂ ᦏᦲᧈᦴ ᦷᦒᦱᧂ ᦑᦙᦲᧃ ᦔᦲᧃ ᦺᦔᦲ ᦵᦔᦙᦲᧂ ᦆᦸᧂ ᦑᦳᧃ ᦵᦟᦙᦲᧂ ᦂᦱᧃ ᦖᦱᧃ ᦂᦲᧈ ᦶᦎᦖᦲ ᦺᦡ ᦕᦲᦰ ᦑᦙᦲᧃ

ᦍᦱᧂ ᦼᦟᦸᧆ ᦵᦖᦙᦲᧆ 《ᦋᦸᧂ ᦉᦳ ᦞᦳᧃ》 ᦟᦲ 《ᦼᦔ ᦐᦲᧈᦖᦲ ᦏᦱᧃ ᦂᦱᦴ》 ᦔᦲᧃ ᦡᦴᧃ ᦼᦂᦖᦲᧃ ᦔᦱᧃ ᦵᦖᦙᦲᧆ ᦔᦱ ᦉᦱ ᦺᦗ

ᦏᦸᧂ ᦷᦒᦳᦖᦲᧃ ᦍᦙᦲᧆ ᦔᦱᧂ ᦂᦳᧃ ᦗᦸᧆ ᦷᦒᦱᧂ ᦺᦔᦲ ᦓᦴ ᦺᦔᦲ ᦐᦱᧃ ᦗᦸᧆ ᦼᦖᦱᧃ ᦵᦉ ᦟᦲ。ᦡᦳᧂ ᦼᦐ ᦞᦙᦲ ᦕᦲᦰ ᦔᦲᧃ ᦗᦲᧈᦸᧂ

ᦺᦔᦲ ᦸᧆᦱᧂ ᦑᦳᧃ, ᦂᦲᧈ ᦶᦎᦖᦲ ᦺᦡ ᦕᦲᦰ ᦷᦂᦸᧃ ᦑᦱᧆ ᦵᦖᦙᦲᧆ ᦔᦳ ᦎᦳᦖᦲ ᦏᦲᧈᧃ ᦋ ᦑᦱᧆ ᦟᦳᧆ ᦖᦱ ᦵᦖᦙᦲᧆ ᦂᦳᧃ,

ᦺᦡ ᦔᦱᦴ ᦑᦖᦲ ᦗᦙᦲᧃ ᦷᦒᦲᧈᦸᧆ ᦉ ᦷᦒᦱᧃ ᦼᦒᦱᧆ, ᦵᦏᦙᦲᧃ ᦵᦂᦙᦲᧂ ᦑᦳᧂ ᦑᦱᧆ ᦖ ᦼᦑ ᦑ ᦐᦱᧂ ᦵᦉ ᦔᦸᧃ ᦔᦱᧂ ᦏᦲᧈᦸ ᦵᦖᦙᦲ

ᦵᦖᦙᦲᧆ ᦔᦳ ᦎᦳᦖᦲ ᦏᦲᧈᧃ, ᦵᦂᦙᦲᧁ ᦡᦴᧃ ᦵᦖᦙᦲᧆ ᦂᦳᧃ ᦟᦲ ᦡᦙᦱᧃ ᦂᦴᧃ ᦏᦲᧈᦳᧃ ᦋᦸᧂ ᦉᦳ ᦞᦳᧃ。ᦵᦐᦱᧁᧃ ᦵᦏᦙᦲᧃ ᦔᦱᧃ

ᦵᦖᦙᦲᧆ ᦂᦱᧂ ᦵᦂᦙᦲᧁᧃ ᦖᦙᦲ ᦉᦳᧆ ᦷᦒᦱᧉ ᦋᦸᧂ ᦉᦳ ᦞᦳᧃ ᦵᦖᦙᦲ ᦆᦸᧂ ᦵᦉᦙᦲᦸ ᦔᦱᦸ ᦋᦱᦸ ᦔᦱᧃ ᦵᦖᦙᦲᧆ ᦵᦉ ᦟᦱᧁ, ᦑᦱᧆ

ᦖ ᦼᦑ ᦑ ᦵᦉ ᦵᦏᦙᦲᧃ ᦆᦴ ᦏᦱᧂ。ᦋᦸ ᦉᦳ ᦞᦳᧃ ᦆᦸᧂ ᦵᦉᦙᦲᦸ ᦺᦔ ᦍ ᦔ ᦑ ᦏᦲᧈᦸ ᦖᦱ ᦵᦉ ᦟᦱᧁ ᦡᦙᦱᧃ ᦼᦗᦸ ᦡᦙᦱᧃ

ᦶᦃᧃ ᦺᦡ ᦆᦴ ᦺᦂᧃ ᦺᦎᧃ ᦐᦱᧂ ᦵᦖ, ᦡᦴᧃ ᦺᦎᦲ ᦔᦱᧃ ᦍᦱ ᦑᦱᦸ ᦟᦲ ᦔᦱᧃ ᦟ ᦉᦙᦲ ᦵᦎᦙᦲᦴᧃ ᦔᦲᧈᦸᧃ, ᦏᦱᧂ ᦟᦳᧃ ᦼᦃ ᦵᦖ

ᦋᦙᦲᧂ ᦺᦔᦲ ᦼᦋᦴᧃ ᦂᦱᧃ。᧒、ᦗᦳᧆ ᦔᦱᧁ ᦖᦙᦲ ᦷᦒᦱᧉ ᦡᦱᦖᦲ ᦷᦒᦙᦲᧁᧃ ᦟᦲ ᦷᦒᦱᧉ ᦔᦱ ᦉᦱ ᦶᦐᦸᧂ ᦟ ᦆ ᦑ ᦶᦋᦸᧂ ᦺᦉ,

ᦶᦔᦱᧁ ᦋᦙᦲᧆ ᦡᦙᦱᧃ ᦷᦂᦸᧃ ᦵᦃᦲᧄ ᦆᦲᧈ ᦡᦴᧃ ᦓᦸᧆ ᦂᦙᦱᧃ ᦂᦱ ᦟᦱ ᦔᦱᧃ ᦵᦖᦙᦲᧆ ᦺᦗ ᦶᦗᦲ。ᦵᦗᦲ ᦖᦱ ᦡᦳᧂ ᦼᦓᧉ ᧑᧒

ᦔᦱᧃ ᦶᦐᦸᧂ ᦗᦳᧆ ᦔᦱᧁ ᦔᦲᧃ ᦏᦲᧈᦴ ᦷᦒᦱᧂ ᦑᦙᦲᧃ ᦵᦔᦙᦲᧂ ᦆᦸᧂ ᦺᦑ ᦑᦳᧃ, ᦺᦑ ᦐᦳᧃ ᦖᦙᦲ ᦂᦱᧃ ᧒ ᦔᦱᧃ ᦉᦖᦲᧃ ᦶᦔᦲᧆ

ᦐᦳᧃᧃ ᦓᦱᦸᧃ ᦗᦳ ᦔᦱᧃ ᦉᦸᧆ ᦂ ᦏᦱᧃ ᦍᦱᧃ ᦒᦱᧃ ᦡᦙᦱᧃ ᦃᦴᦰ ᦖᦙᦲ ᦃ ᦡᦱ ᦔᦸᧃ ᦂᦲᧈ ᦃᦴᦰ ᦼᦃᦸᧁᧃ ᦃᦱᧂ, ᦡᦳᧃ ᦏᦱᧂ ᦷᦒᦱᧂ

ᦶᦎᦖᦲ ᦷᦂᦸᧃ ᦡ ᧐᧐ ᦑᦙᦲ ᦏᦱᧂ ᦆᦲᧈ ᦡᦴᧃ ᦓᦸᧆ ᦂᦙᦱᧃ ᦔᦱ ᦉᦱ ᦺᦗ, ᦷᦂᦙᦱᧃ ᦍᦸᧆ ᦖᦙᦲ ᦡᦳᧂ ᦼᦓᧉ ᦔᦱᧃ ᧗ ᦶᦎᦖᦲ

ᦵᦟᦙᦲᧂ ᦂᦱᧃ ᦃᦴᦰ ᦑᦱ ᦀᦲᧈᧃ ᦏᦱᧃ ᦍᦱᧃ, ᦆᦸ ᦗᦱᧃᧃ ᦼᦆᧁ ᦉ ᦷᦒᦱᧂ ᦑᦸᧆ ᦡᦴᧃ ᦂᦱᧆ ᦷᦒᦴᧃ, ᦼᦎ ᧗ ᦡᦸᧆ ᦡᦙᦲᧃ,

ᦼᦎ ᧗ ᦔᦸ ᦞᦙᦲ ᦔᦸᧆ ᦷᦒᦱᦲ ᦆᦴ ᦡᦴᧃ, ᦔᦳᦖᦲ ᦷᦒᦱᧂ ᦑᦸᧆ ᦶᦀᦸᧁ ᦟᦲᧈᦖᦲ ᦟᦲ ᦷᦂᦸᧆ ᦂᦖᦲ ᦆᦴ ᦡᦙᦱᧃ ᦂᦱᧃ ᦔᦲᧃ ᦉᦴᦰ ᦼᦒᦳᦸᧁ

ᦀᦲᧈᧃ ᦺᦋ ᦶᦗᦲ ᦟᦲ。᧓、ᦗᦳᧆ ᦔᦱᧁ ᦑᦙᦲᧃ ᦡᦙᦱᧃ ᦗᦙᦲᧃ ᦷᦒᦸᧁ ᦉᦱᧂ ᦗᦱᧆ ᦟᦲ ᦗᦙᦲᧃ ᦏᦱᧃ ᦍᦱᧃ ᦉᦙᦲᦴᧃ ᦗᦱᧂ ᦀᦸ ᦞ ᦑ ᦔᦱ ᦉᦱ

ᦺᦗ。ᦵᦍᦙᦲᧂ ᦑᦙᦲᧂ, ᦟᦱᧆ ᦵᦏᦸᧁ ᦖᦱᧃ ᦉᦙᦲᦴᧃ ᦕᦲᦰ ᦟᦱᧁ ᦒ ᦖ ᦀᦲ ᦒᦱ ᦶᦎᦖᦲ ᦡᦳᧂ ᦏᦱᧂ ᦼᦟᦸᧆ ᦵᦖᦙᦲᧆ ᦔᦱ

ᦉᦱ ᦺᦗ ᦶᦐᦸᧂ “ᦼᦒᦸᧁ ᦡᦲᧈᦴ ᦒᦙᦲᧃ ᦺᦉ、ᦎᦱᦖᦲ ᦺᦋ” , ᦶᦎᦖᦲ ᦡᦳᧂ ᦼᦓᧉ ᦔᦸᧃ ᦃᦴᦰ ᦶᦓᦸᧁ ᦂᦴ ᧐᧐ ᦟᦱ、

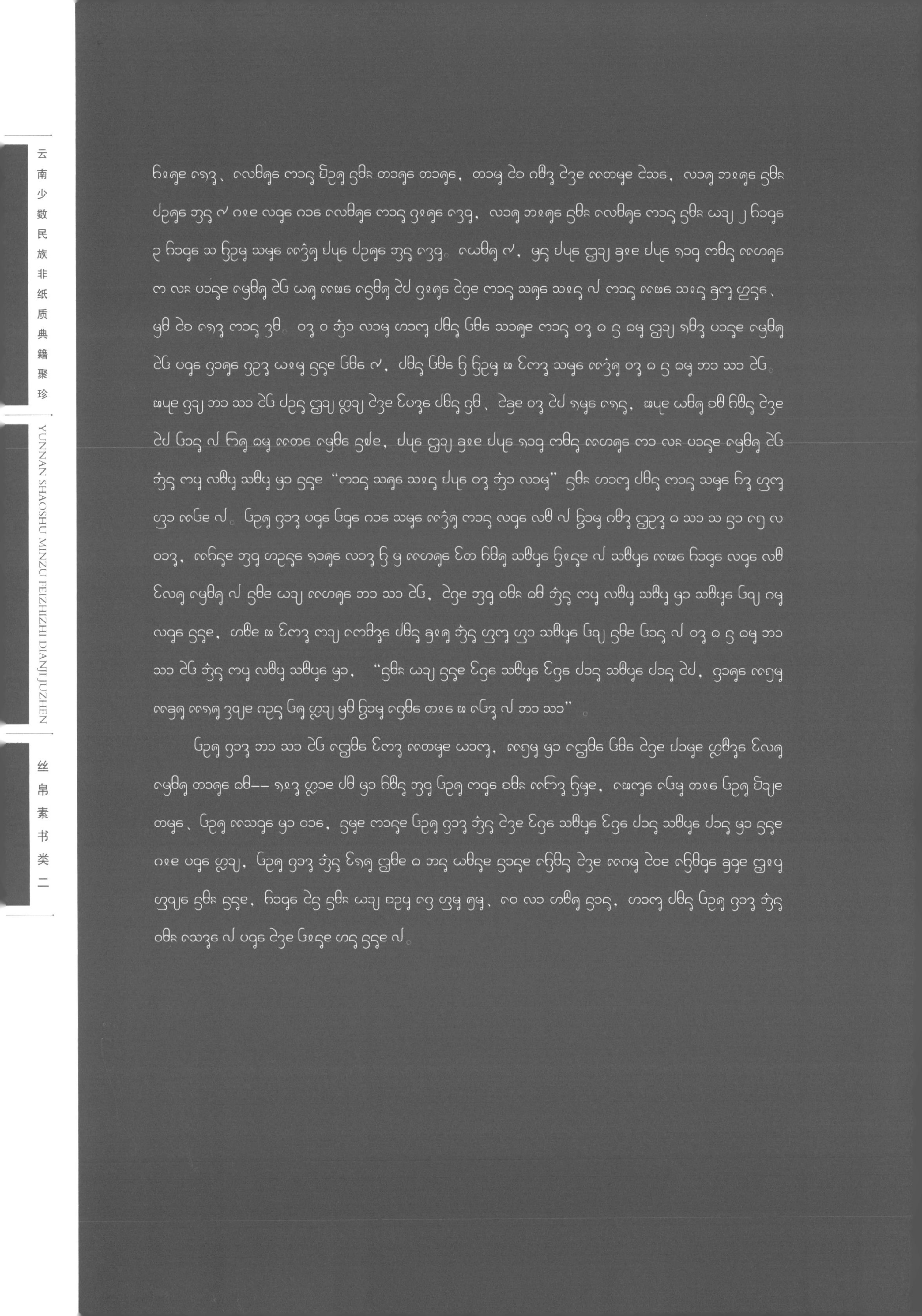

[illegible]

[illegible]

布画故事幡

布画故事幡
年代：19 世纪
尺寸：长 630 厘米，宽 48 厘米
收藏单位：云南省博物馆

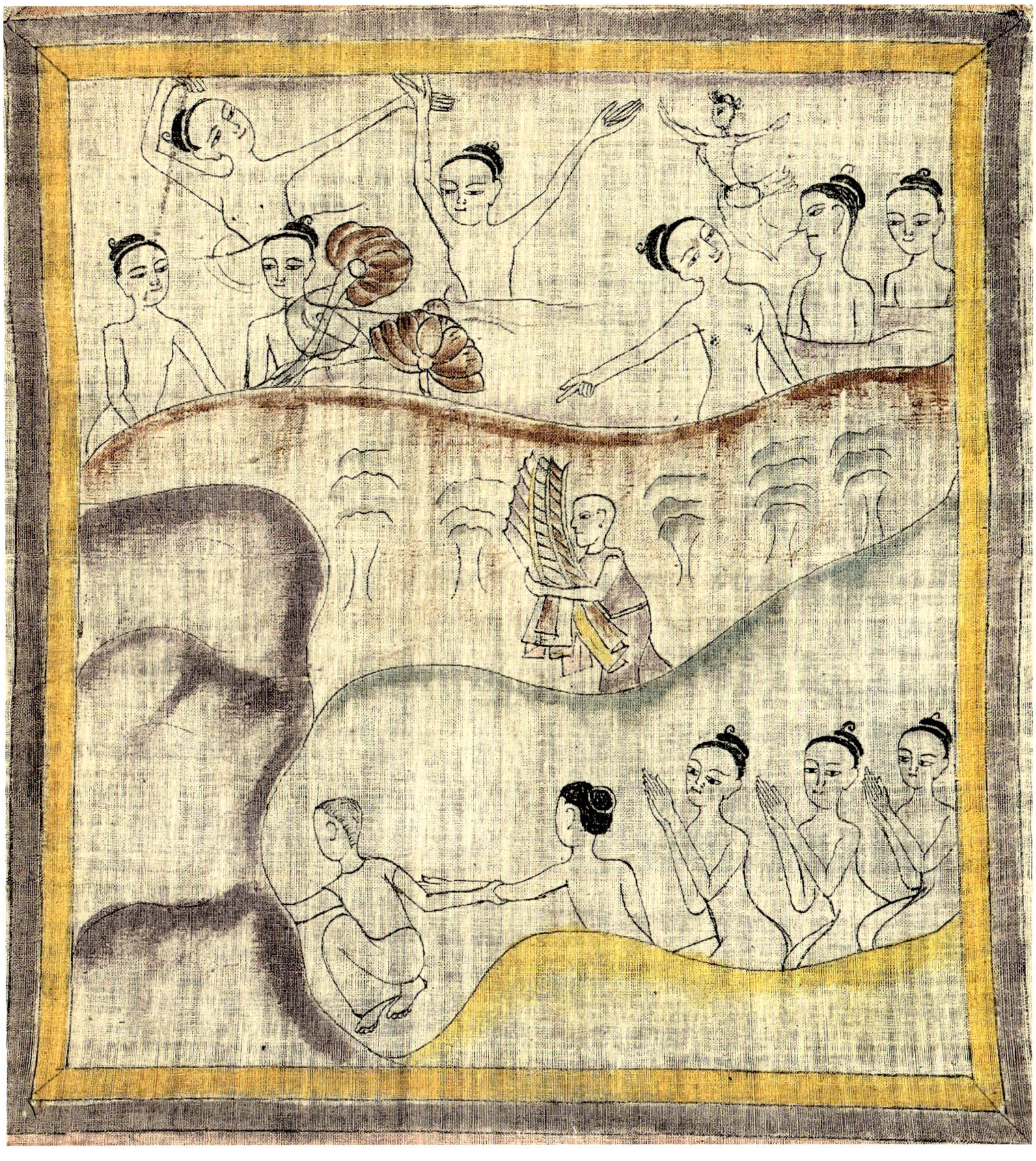

后记

我们长期从事云南少数民族古籍的抢救保护、翻译整理和出版规划工作，对云南少数民族古籍的分布、储量和传承现状有一个基本的了解，发现各民族都拥有或历史上曾经拥有过一些载体独特、形式各异的非纸质典籍，全面抢救保护、搜集整理这些分布零散、濒临消失且长期不被关注的少数民族非纸质典籍是一项具有重要意义的文化工程。

2015年初，我们便逐步对各民族的非纸质典籍开展专题调查，不断征集线索、采集古籍图片，随着资料的不断累积，便萌生了将非纸质典籍专题影印出版的想法。这个想法得到云南人民出版社的大力支持，经申报入选“国家民文出版项目库”，并获民族文字出版专项资金的经费支持，为编纂出版本书创造了有利的条件。2017年，本书主创团队参与云南大学周琼教授主持的国家社会科学基金重大项目“中国西南少数民族灾害文化数据库建设”，进一步推动了本项目的执行。

抢救保护承载着丰富民族文化内涵的云南少数民族非纸质典籍，具有重要的意义，也是一个充满挑战和未知的尝试。全面搜集云南各少数民族的非纸质典籍是一项耗时、费钱、费力的工作，这些典籍东一本西一样地散布在全省各地，从线索征集到一一获得授权采集图片确实经历了各种波折。有的图片在采集过程中受自然条件的限制，采集难度较大。特别是金石铭刻类的图片，有的稍模糊，或缺乏全景图，甚是遗憾。图片如愿采集回来了，要将这些琳琅满目的典籍进行鉴别、释读、分类更是一项艰巨的任务，没有统一的划分标准可以参照，没有现成的经验可资借鉴，我们唯有摸着石头过河。进入统稿、编排环节，我们既要考虑覆盖云南各世居少数民族，又要考虑丛书的体量、编排等，取舍两难，着实让人困扰。最后，我们唯有以抢救保护、搜集整理少数民族古籍资料为出发点，以云南少数民族非纸质典籍的文化价值作为评判标准，以期为社会科学研究、文化产业发展等提供可资借鉴的材料。就收录范围，我们采用广义的民族古籍概念，适当突破民族古籍学学科的界定和范围，各民族的金石铭刻、骨刻、丝帛素书、竹木简牍等都是我们收录的对象。就典籍的考释和图解，目前学界对各民族古籍的搜集整理、研究程度参差不齐，对古籍的翻译整理和释读等亦有巨大差距。如对纳西族非纸质典籍的收集、研究起步较早，我们基本可以释读典籍的名称和内容。但彝族、壮族、藏族、傣族等民族的非纸质典籍研究尚处于起步阶段，释读、命名尚有难度，如壮族的骨刻书，我们知道是用于历算的，但具体的内涵、使用方法尚未形成统一定论，我们实不敢妄解。所以部分非纸质典籍的文字说明略显简单粗陋。

本项目得到了云南人民出版社的大力支持和配合，特别是金学丽编审在项目策划、调研、稿件甄选、编辑等方面倾注了很多的心血，为项目的顺利开展做出了巨大的努力。吴贵飙馆长、普学旺译审、谢沫华研究馆员、起国庆研究馆员、张金文主任在项目申报、执行等方面给予了切实可行的指导意见和帮助。

本书资料的收集，得到丽江市东巴文化研究院、丽江市博物院、丽江玉龙纳西族自治县图书馆、文山壮族苗族自治州民族宗教事务委员会等基层民族古籍工作部门的全力支持和配合，得到李德静、牛增裕、木琛、李瑞山、王明富、和丽宝、赵庆莲、汉刚、胡文明等专家的鼎力相助，谨致谢意。

为较好地呈现这套丛书，我们多方求证、全面搜集典籍、认真编排，确实做了很多切实的努力。但鉴于本书的执行、撰稿人员以青年学者居多，书稿难免有考虑不周和不当之处，敬请读者批评指正！

本书编委会

2022 年 10 月修订

Postscript

We have been engaging in the rescue, protection, translation, sorting and publication planning of ancient books and records of ethnic minorities in Yunnan for a long time, and have a basic understanding on the distribution, reserves and inheritance status of ancient books and records of ethnic minorities in Yunnan. We find that all the ethnic minorities have or once had some non-paper ancient books and records with unique carriers and various forms in history. It is a cultural project of great significance to comprehensively rescue, protect, collect and sort out these scattered non-paper ancient books and records of ethnic minorities that are on the verge of disappearance and have not been drawing attention to for a long time.

We began to conduct special investigations on non-paper ancient books and records of various ethnic minorities, and are constantly collecting clues and pictures of ancient books and records since the beginning of 2015. With the continuous accumulation of data, we came up with the idea of photocopying and publishing special subjects of non-paper ancient books and records. This idea was vigorously supported by Yunnan People's Publishing House, and it was selected into the "national project library for publication of ethnic books and records" through application. Besides, it was also supported by the special fund for the publication of the ethnic books and records, and has created favorable conditions for compilation and publication of this book. In 2017, the creative team of this project participated in "the Establishment of the Database for Disaster Culture in the Ethnic Minorities in Southeast China" (Approval Number of the Project: 17ZDA158) which is the major project of the national social science foundation, and vigorously promoted the implementation of this series of books.

It is of great significance to rescue and protect the non-paper ancient books and records of ethnic minorities in Yunnan, which carries over rich ethnic cultural connotations, and is also an attempt full of challenges and mysteries. It is a time-consuming, costly and arduous task to collect all the non-paper ancient books and records of ethnic minorities in Yunnan. These ancient books and records are widely scattered all over the province. Relevant working personnel have experienced various twists and turns from collecting the clues to obtaining the authorization to collect pictures one by one. Restricted by the natural conditions, some pictures are difficult to take. In particular, the inscription pictures are slightly blurred or lack of panoramic images. What a pity! At last, the pictures were collected as expected. It is an arduous task to identify, interpret and classify these dazzling records. There is no unified classification standard to refer to and no ready-made experience to base on. We have to grope our way. In terms of compilation and arrangement, not only should we consider the coverage of ethnic minorities living in Yunnan, but also we should take the volume and arrangement of the series of books into account. It is really confusing to make choices. Finally, we can only take the rescue, protection, collection and sorting-out of the ancient books and records of ethnic minorities as the starting point, and the cultural value of non-paper ancient books and records of ethnic minorities in Yunnan as the evaluation standard, so as to provide reference materials for social science research and cultural industry development. In terms of the scope of inclusions, we adopt the broad concept of ethnic ancient books and records and appropriately break through the definition and scope of ethnic ancient books and records. Inscriptions, bone carvings, silk books and bamboo and wooden engravings of various ethnic minorities are all included in our collection scope. The lower limit of time of the ancient books and records collected is uniformly fixed as prior to 1949. In terms of the interpretations and illustrations of ancient books and records, collection, collation and research on ancient books and records of various ethnic minorities are at different levels, and there is a huge gap in the translation, collation and interpretation of ancient books and records. For instance, due to early start of the collection and research on the Naxi non-paper ancient books and records, we can basically read names and contents of the ancient books and records. However, the research on non-paper ancient books and records of the Yi, Zhuang, Tibetan, Dai and other ethnic minorities is still in the initial stage, and it is difficult to read and name them. For example, we know that the bone carvings of the Zhuang Ethnic Minority are used for calendar calculation, but no unified conclusion has been reached on their specific connotation and method of use. We don't dare to make improper interpretations. Therefore, some of the explanatory notes on the non-paper ancient books are slightly simple and not so detailed.

This project has received vigorous support and cooperation from Yunnan People's Publishing House. In particular, Senior Editor Jin Xueli has spared no efforts in project planning, research, manuscript selections and editing, and made a great contribution to the smooth development of the project. Director Wu Guibiao, senior translator Pu Xuewang, Research librarian Xie Mohua, Qi Guoqing and Zhang Jinwen have provided practical guidance and help in the project application, implementation and other aspects.

Data collections for this book has been completely supported and cooperated by the Research Institute of Dongba Culture of Lijiang, the Library of Yulong Naxi Autonomous County of Lijiang, the Affairs Bureau of Ethnic and Religious Affairs of Zhuang-Miao Autonomous Prefecture of Wenshan and other grass-roots departments of ethnic ancient books and records. We would like to express our gratitude to Li Dejing, Niu Zengyu, Mu Chen, Li Ruishan, Wang Mingfu, He Libao, Zhao Qinglian, Han Gang, Hu Wenming and other experts.

We have made lots of practical efforts in seeking confirmations from various sources, comprehensively collecting ancient books and records and making arrangements carefully, so as to better present this series of books. However, since the book is mainly collected and compiled by young scholars, it is hard to avoid making incomprehensive and improper considerations. We are looking forward to your criticism and corrections!

Editorial Board of the Book

October, 2022